NINA SIMONE

Icons of Pop Music

Series Editors: Jill Halstead, The Grieg Academy, University of Bergen,
and Dave Laing, independent writer and broadcaster

Books in this series, designed for undergraduates and the general reader,
offer a critical profile of a key figure or group in twentieth-century pop
music. These short volumes focus on the work rather than on biography,
and emphasize critical interpretation.

Published

The Velvet Underground
Richard Witts

Bob Dylan
Keith Negus

Elvis Costello
Dai Griffiths

Björk
Nicola Dibben

Buddy Holly
Dave Laing

James Brown
John Scannell

Brian Wilson
Kirk Curnutt

Forthcoming

Elton John
Dave Laing

Joni Mitchell
Jill Halstead

The Beatles
Ian Inglis

Elvis Presley
Mark Duffett

NINA SIMONE

RICHARD ELLIOTT

Equinox Publishing Ltd

Sheffield, UK   Bristol, CT

Published by Equinox Publishing Ltd

UK: Unit S3, Kelham House, 3 Lancaster Street, Sheffield S3 8AF

USA: ISD, 70 Enterprise Drive, Bristol, CT 06010

www.equinoxpub.com

British Library Cataloguing-in-Publication Data
A catalogue record for this book is available from the British Library.

ISBN-13   978 1 84553 988 7   (paperback)

Library of Congress Cataloging-in-Publication Data

Elliott, Richard, 1971 June 28–
   Nina Simone / Richard Elliott.
        pages cm. -- (Icons of pop music)
   Includes bibliographical references and index.
   ISBN 978-1-84553-988-7 (pb)
1. Simone, Nina, 1933-2003. 2. Singers--Biography. I. Title.
   ML420.S5635E45 2013
   782.42164092--dc23
   [B]
                                                        2012046460

Typeset by Atheus
Printed and bound by Lightning Source, La Vergne, TN, USA

Contents

Acknowledgements

I am grateful for comments by Richard Middleton and David Clarke on earlier versions of some of this material and to David for suggesting I write a book on Nina Simone. Thanks are also due to Jill Halstead and Dave Laing, editors of the Icons of Pop Music series, for their enthusiastic response to the initial book proposal and their subsequent comments as the manuscript developed. During the initial review process, I also received additional anonymous reader comments which helped me to focus the book's scope and to consider issues relating to Simone's life and work. While restructuring the book along its current pattern, I benefited from comments by Nanette de Jong, who also provided invaluable encouragement and support. Much of the information and many of the thoughts contained within this text were developed while teaching the postgraduate courses 'Studying Popular Musics' and 'Popular Music and the Politics of Authenticity' between 2009 and 2012 and I remain indebted to the students who took those classes and contributed to a range of fascinating debates. Eunsun Chung's support while undertaking research for this book was invaluable and our shared love of Nina Simone's music fuelled a number of observations that made their way into the text. Conversations with Lars Iyer on the subject of Simone, jazz, blues and late voices fed into the discussion of lateness in Chapter 4 and continue to inform my current work. Discussions with Elodie Roy on time, memory, nostalgia, writing and much more have inspired and encouraged me. Thanks to the Da Mata family for providing much needed time and space for thinking and writing at a crucial time. Peter and Angela Elliott read sections of the manuscript and offered feedback and Maria Mata heard me out through numerous iterations of the themes and structure of the book; for these acts of patience, and much more, I remain thankful. I'd like to extend gratitude to Val Hall for her coordination of the publication process and to Sarah Norman for project managing the copyediting stage.

Introduction

In 2003, the year of Nina Simone's death, a version of her song 'Sinnerman', remixed by Felix da Housecat, was released on the second *Verve Remixed* album. *Verve Remixed* is a project that involves contemporary reworking of tracks from the label's extensive archive of jazz and blues recordings. Simone's work was a prominent feature of the early volumes in the series, with 'Sinnerman' being the most widely circulated via a range of club mixes. The track begins with a dance beat that gives no melodic clue as to the identity of the song until 45 seconds in, at which point clued-up jazz, soul or gospel fans will likely recognize the rolling piano riff that emerges as that which drives Simone's 1965 recording of 'Sinnerman'. Beat and riff continue as if locked together for another half a minute before the beat drops away to leave the piano to do its work. When the beat re-enters we start to hear fragments of Simone's voice, asking "Where you gonna run to?" repeatedly, then "Oh Sinnerman, where you gonna run to?" At nearly three minutes we escape the loop, Simone's deep, sensual voice emoting as she imagines some imminent day of reckoning. Then we are back into repetition again, the voice becoming a fetishized object amid the rolling piano and disco beats, riding the groove to the song's conclusion. 'Sinnerman', which Simone introduced to her audience as a song she learned at religious revival meetings during her North Carolina childhood, thus makes its long journey from one ritual space (the church) to another (the nightclub), from one congregation to another, and from a time before the artist was born to the posthumous moment in which she became "the late Nina Simone".

Another example of Simone's "lateness" can be found by going back to a moment when she was alive but, in many ways, invisible. It is the video for 'My Baby Just Cares For Me' directed by Peter Lord for Aardman Animations in 1987. The song, originally recorded in the late 1950s, had become a hit following its use in an advert for Chanel earlier in the year and it was clearly felt that a video was needed to accompany the track. Lord's video showed the song being sung by a Claymation cat standing at a microphone, while the famous descending piano figure that instantly earmarked the version as Simone's was played by a different Claymation creature.

What was notable in both these moments was the absence of Nina Simone herself; only her voice seemed to remain, and even that was disembodied through the mediations of sampling and animation. It is common following the death of an artist that we revisit their life through their work and our memories of prior encounters with that work. With the loss of recording artists this process is aided by the recorded artefacts themselves, which provide voices with an afterlife. But it is not only recordings that bring voices back from the dead; cover versions, remixes and new contexts promise to breathe new life into late voices. Felix's 'Sinnerman' sends its invitation to a new generation of potential Nina Simone fans, as do the Chanel advert and the Claymation video. The latter is my earliest memory of hearing Nina Simone and I recall the song being everywhere that year. But where was Nina Simone herself? Neither in the advert nor the video, where her role was further reduced by the suggestion that singer and pianist were separate entities, when in fact they were one and the same woman.

Those willing to look back at that career would discover the Nina Simone of the 1960s, of 'Mississippi Goddam', 'Four Women' and 'To Be Young, Gifted and Black'. These were her songs but she also made other people's songs her own, selecting from the established songbooks of Cole Porter and George Gershwin and the newly emerging songbooks of Bob Dylan, Leonard Cohen, and the Gibb brothers. This was the Nina Simone of the civil rights era, her songs a vital soundtrack to that historic moment. Then came silence and exile, as Simone left a US she believed would never be cured of racism for successive exiles in Barbados, Liberia, Switzerland, the Netherlands and France. Though she continued to perform, record and sell records, her work fell off the critical radar.

Nina Simone was a performer who received a great deal of attention during her heyday in the 1960s but relatively little within the Anglophone world in the later stages of her career. She continued to be revered in France – the country in which she lived for the last years of her life – and had a brief boost to her career in the United Kingdom following the success of 'My Baby Just Cares For Me' in the 1980s. In her later years, when she was written about, it tended to be in terms that emphasized her successful past and difficult present. There is still a surprising absence of commentary on Simone and her work in general accounts of blues, jazz, soul and other forms of black music;

this is also true of scholarly work on music and gender. However, Simone's later life was also a time of profound reflection for the artist and, for anyone involved in researching her life and work, her late period provides some invaluable documents. The early 1990s saw the publication of her autobiography, *I Put a Spell on You*, the release of a documentary of her career (a French production entitled *La Légende*) and a new studio album. While most of these documents concerned themselves with her past they were all narrated in what I call her "late voice". I will have more to say about the late voice further on, but for now we might think of it as a voice that attempts to connect history as it really was with memory as it is now, often leading to history as it should have been. Simone attempted her reconciliation with history as it really was by moving away from the site of her disappointment. She came to be seen as a performer who was unable, unwilling or – as she herself would see it – denied the opportunity to rescale the heights of her 1960s heyday. While pursuing her own memory work – her increasingly nostalgic songs, her autobiographical projects – she became subject to the memory work of her audience, who looked back to that same heyday.

A Recorded Life

While the biographical details of any artist whose work gathers a substantial audience are likely to be attached, in one form or another, to presentations and explanations of the work, there are some artists who seem to attract the conflation of art and life more than others. Nina Simone was one of these artists and there are few accounts of her music that omit some sort of reference to certain traumatic experiences in her early life, to her connection to the civil rights movement, or to her often troubled later years.

Despite the relative exclusion of Simone from general works on black music, the years since her death have witnessed a growing interest in her life and career. A number of biographies have appeared (Cohodas 2010; Hampton and Nathan 2004; Acker 2004; Brun-Lambert 2009), as have scholarly articles addressing her role in the civil rights movement (Berman 2004; Feldstein 2005; Kernodle 2008; Brooks 2011). This book draws upon all these sources, and on Simone's own account of her life (Simone and Cleary 2003), while placing greater emphasis on the interpretation of music from across the artist's entire career. My account of Simone's music offers a hermeneutics of her work that connects to parallel histories, concepts and theories. The book explicitly addresses what some authors regard as the problem of reading Simone's work through reference to her life and its socio-historical context, as opposed to viewing the work primarily from an aesthetic perspective. Ultimately it argues that these factors should not be separated but that it is important that questions regarding their relationship be constantly raised, if only to maintain a focus on the quality of Simone's work as a musician. Too often she is regarded only as a "symptom of history" (Caruth 1995, 5), both a product of the cultural trauma into which she was born and a slave to her own mental condition (Simone had been taking medication for bipolar disorder for much of her later career, a fact that only came to public attention following the artist's death and which may help to explain some of the capricious behaviour for which she was well known). Simone cannot be discussed without reference to these vital influences but she should not be reduced to them.

Another original element of this book is its proposal of a theory of the "late voice", a concept which refers both to biography and to aesthetics. The late voice, it is argued, is both something that can be discussed in terms of work carried out late in an artist's career and an aesthetic strategy which artists can deploy at any stage in their work and which, in fact, can often be detected in the early work of many. Nina Simone is hardly unique in this respect but she is an exemplary representative of the late voice in that her work is characterized by an emphasis on experience, loss, memory, disappointment, yearning and nostalgia. The concept of the late voice will be put forward as one way of navigating the problem of weighing up biographical, aesthetic and textual accounts of performers and their work.

It may seem to be stating the obvious to want to consider Simone as a black woman, yet very few books on music and race or music and gender have given more than passing reference to her. In the broader sphere of popular music studies, Simone is also under-represented, for a number of possible reasons. One of these is the often-cited difficulty in categorizing her music; she should not feature in books on blues or jazz because, it is argued, she was not strictly speaking a blues or jazz singer; a similar line of reasoning applies to works on soul and folk music. And, while Simone is associated in the popular imagination with the civil rights movement, the more rarefied area of civil rights scholarship often ignores her, seeing her as someone whose pop star status prevented her from fully engaging with activism. This book will argue that it is important to prevent Simone's departure from the history of popular music and the wider culture.

The usefulness of connecting authorial biography and artistic output was the subject of much debate during the time period this book covers and, while there is not sufficient space here to discuss the work of Roland Barthes, Michel Foucault and Jacques Derrida, these and other figures have influenced a number of the interpretations offered in this book. Should these figures be seen to be operating in, or reflecting on, a world and an experience that are quantitatively or qualitatively different from that experienced by Simone (and such criticisms are not unusual: see, for example, Rose 1994, 198–9 n.24; for a refutation, see Middleton 2006, 282 n.108), I should point out that my interpretations have also been influenced by theorists such as Farah Jasmine Griffin (2001, 2004), Hortense Spillers (2003) and Alexander Weheliye (2002, 2005), all of whom draw upon poststructuralist thought to elucidate black American art.

Another criticism that could be levelled at the use of Simone's biography to explain her art is to be found in the ways in which identity is occasionally wielded as a potentially essentialist and universalizing discourse. An example which Simone herself highlighted was the frequency with which she was compared to other black female singers – most obviously Billie Holiday – because of her race and gender. In her autobiography, Simone suggests that this happened because of her early success with 'I Loves You, Porgy', a song previously associated with Holiday:

> Calling me a jazz singer was a way of ignoring my musical background because I didn't fit into white ideas of what a black performer should be. It was a racist thing: "If she's black she must be a jazz singer." It diminished me, exactly like Langston Hughes was diminished when people called him a "great black poet". Langston was a great poet period and it was up to him and him alone to say what part the colour of his skin had to do with that (Simone and Cleary 2003, 69).

The last point Simone makes here is interesting in that it allows a certain amount of space for self-essentialization, or, as it has been defined in theories of identity politics, strategic essentialization (a concept I will return to in Chapter 2). Simone displays a strategic deployment of the word "jazz" when she writes, just prior to the passage quoted above, that "the black man in America was jazz in everything he did – in the way he walked, talked, thought and acted . . . so in that sense because I was black I was a jazz singer" (68–9). A similar slipperiness about the use of the word "soul" will be considered later in this book, at which point debates concerning art, identity and essentialization will be considered (at least to an extent allowable in a short work on a specific artist) with reference to work by Griffin, Robin Kelley and others.

Whatever one's feelings about theory, aesthetics and biography, the fact remains that no one has yet produced a convincing account of Simone's work without recourse to her published autobiography, even those who dismiss it as "contrived" and "sterilized" (Brun-Lambert 2009, 329). Most commentators (including Brun-Lambert) would maintain that *I Put a Spell on You* remains a vital contribution to her work, just as Billie Holiday's *Lady Sings the Blues* or Charles Mingus's *Beneath the Underdog* do to theirs. It is undeniably performative and should perhaps be read as an open text, with readers allowed to make connections rather than taking what Simone says as gospel. And if that word, used here to signify truth, takes on other resonances when applied to music, we should remain alive to the ways in which truth is discovered and performed in musical traditions. Gospel can be seen to highlight a distinction between "truth" (something fixed) and what we might call "truthing" (an ongoing process). By making such a distinction I am partly alluding to Christopher Small's (1998) concept of "musicking", wherein something that is generally thought of as a thing ("music") is recognized instead as a process ("musicking"). But just as music, despite Small's protestations, remains a thing, so we must think of truth as at least the perception of a thing, as truth itself. Both truth, and the processes of fidelity or faith that follow from its recognition, find one of their more sophisticated philosophical interpretations in the work of Alain Badiou (2005), another continental reference point for this book. The epiphanic moment of "coming through" that is to be found in the religious tradition in which Simone was raised finds its philosophic analogue in Badiou's theory of "event". Just as the recognition of, and subsequent commitment to, religious truth is a subjectivizing process (a process, in other words, through which subjects learn to live in the world), so other "events" and "fidelity to events" promote particular responses and ways of being in the world.

At the same time we need to balance biographical, artist-centred accounts with reference to the social world in which such artists operate. As Ingrid Monson points out, the discographical and biographical work that has helped to establish and maintain the idea of jazz as a vital modern art form has also led, at times, to an over-emphasis on individual genius (2007, 5–6). An approach that takes account of socio-historical events and contexts can therefore help to explain the development of certain cultural practices, including music. To take one example, Monson notes how jazz emerged within the "structural condition" of Jim Crow racism in the USA (2007, 6). Monson's account of jazz connects to what Richard Peterson has called the "production of culture" model, in which greater emphasis is placed upon the factors which shape, determine and "routinize" the conditions under which cultural innovators can emerge than upon the lives and works of the innovators themselves. Peterson (1990) has made use of the production of culture perspective to explain the reasons for the emergence of rock 'n' roll in the mid-1950s, pointing out that an understanding of this cultural event requires an understanding of the various structuring conditions (social, legal, occupational, technological, and so on) that allowed innovators such as Elvis Presley, Chuck Berry, Little Richard and Jerry Lee Lewis to attain exposure and popularity. As I have suggested elsewhere, it is necessary to balance such accounts, which provide a sober alternative to biography-based rock histories, with recognition of the ongoing power of more populist, or even mythical, accounts (Elliott 2008b).

It is also important to highlight the ways in which the structuring processes of social factors, as understood by theories of musicking or the production of culture, intersect with, and derive their power and meaning from, concrete individual cases. Many of the most convincing accounts of individual musical performances are the result of combining the social and the individual in hermeneutical procedures that do justice to both individual and collective, cause and effect, call and response. Samuel Floyd, for example, provides a useful way to read a range of musical performances via the concept of "cultural memory". For Floyd, cultural memory refers to "nonfactual and non-referential motivations, actions, and beliefs that members of a culture seem, without direct knowledge or deliberate training to 'know' – that feel unequivocally 'true' and 'right' when encountered, experienced and executed" (1995, 8). The moment of execution or practice momentarily fixes the memory, but the memory is as much an action, or process, as it is an object or target being searched for. This emphasis on the moment and the process does not contradict other accounts such as Small's (far from it), but it does allow us to link the individual example with collective conditioning and to allow the notion of the object (in the form of the archive or repository) to retain its importance. For, as well as being a live process, cultural memory is also "a repository of meanings that comprise the subjective knowledge of a people, its immanent thoughts, its structures, and its practices; these thoughts, structures, and practices are transferred and understood unconsciously but become conscious and culturally objective in practice and perception" (Floyd 1995, 8).

We might think of cultural memory, then, as a form of awareness possessed by individuals within a society which encompasses the intuitive and the experienced, the general and the specific, the known and the felt. Such awareness attaches itself to a signifying community and relies on both memory and politics for its continuation. Floyd's account of cultural memory can be usefully placed alongside the "social memory" described by James Fentress and Chris Wickham. For these authors, social memory functions as "a source of knowledge" and

> does more than provide a set of categories through which, in an unselfconscious way, a group experiences its surroundings; it also provides the group with material for conscious reflection. This means that we must situate groups in relation to their own traditions, asking how they interpret their own "ghosts", and how they use them as a source of knowledge (1992, 26; see also Elliott 2011).

In what follows, I bring together the concepts of cultural memory (aligned with cultural trauma) and the event to consider the ways in which Nina Simone's life and work can be read as both response and contribution to the ongoing cultural memory of black experience in the United States. As for the ways in which the personal interacts with the public and cultural, I wish to take my lead from Simone herself. Throughout her public career, Simone referred to herself and her work via references to "my people". This assertion of belonging, and of shared trauma, was and remains central to any understanding of Simone's art, even (and perhaps especially) at those moments where she moved as far away from public engagement as she could. A product of, and contributor to, the second-wave feminism that asserted itself during the 1960s, Simone remained a woman for whom the personal was always political.

For us as readers and auditors of Simone's life and work, there should not be too much guilt in drawing connections between her work and that of Billie Holiday, Bessie Smith, or other black female precursors, contemporaries or successors. Nor should we flinch from connecting her to the troubles and traumas of her time, or considering the role her own split personality had on her work. It was arguably that split that enabled her to maintain seemingly opposing attitudes towards the role of identity politics in her career, one minute asserting herself as a representative of a black female subjectivity born of historical trauma, the next claiming that all there was to know about her could be found in her music alone. We do not experience Nina Simone in a vacuum any more than we experience any other person's life and work in a context-free manner. We create our Nina Simones from the tapestry of fact, confession, myth, art and critical (and non-critical) discourse that has been made available for us and which we renew with each proclamation.

In this book I weave in and out of that tapestry, hopefully adding some new threads and patterns of my own. The book is broadly structured on a chronological basis and divided into five sections: Categories, Politics, Possession, Lateness and Legacy. While each section allows a focus on particular themes and issues in Simone's work, the mapping of each onto a particular chronology should be seen primarily as a pragmatic exercise, a framing device that hopefully allows for a coherent retelling of the Nina Simone story. Defiant as Simone may have been towards any attempt to pin her down or label her, we have to organize our memories of her life and legacy in some manner, though we should also be wary of over-simplification. Just as Simone was political in one form or another all of her working life, she also remained uncategorizable. There are as many parallels between her earliest work and her latest as there are paradoxes. Many of the things that could be said for *The Amazing Nina Simone* (one of her first studio albums, from 1959) could be said for *A Single Woman* (her last, from 1993). That the categories I have chosen are overlapping *and* interdependent should be kept in mind.

In my discussion of Simone's recorded legacy, I start at the beginning (her first official recordings) and finish somewhere near the end. I say "somewhere near" because it is harder to ascertain the end than the beginning. If I am concentrating on recordings, should the end be her last recorded album? What of the fact that Simone continued to perform for more than a decade after that album and that many (most?) of these performances were recorded in some form or another via bootleg audio recordings, television broadcasts, videos, DVDs and, more recently, amateur video recordings posted to video-sharing websites? Or that previously unissued recordings are regularly unearthed in the process of producing compilation albums, box sets and reissues of studio albums (for example, the remastered version of *A Single Woman* that was released in 2008 with bonus cuts including Simone's take on Prince's 'Sign O' the Times' amidst other delights)? Or that her recorded legacy continues to inspire new recordings by contemporary artists, some of which sample, remix or otherwise include Simone's own voice (not only those remixes mentioned at the outset, but also Lisa "Simone" Stroud's inclusion of a duet performed by mother and daughter on the latter's *Simone on Simone* album)? As Michel Foucault (1979) noted, it is always difficult to decide on what constitutes an artist's meaningful work when engaged in the posthumous work of analysis.

But if the end is hard to fix, the in-between of Simone's recorded work is even more so. It is not that we are unable to organize her work into chronologically ordered releases and even eras – a discography is provided at the end of the book to help with this – but rather that Simone's tendency to employ multiple styles, genres and voices, and to revisit and reinterpret material over the course of her career, means that any attempt to describe a particular performance inevitably leads one to think about another performance from earlier or later in the artist's career. For example, although I base my initial discussion of categorization in Chapter 1 on Simone's recordings for the Colpix label, I also make reference to work released later in her career by Philips and RCA. To attempt to do otherwise, I found, is to make life unnecessarily difficult.

As to the choice of which recordings from Simone's large catalogue to discuss, I have selected examples that, in my opinion, represent the five perspectives from which I am viewing Simone's work. For the first chapter, I have selected a number of performances that show how we might attempt to categorize that work generically and stylistically. At the same time, recognizing the difficulty of categorizing this particular artist, I provide discussions that problematize the easy division of songs into styles and genres, often by considering what Simone does with particular songs and what other artists have done with the same or similar source material. In discussing politics, I initially choose some of the most obviously political of Simone's songs, then proceed to open up the ways in which we might define and categorize political music. For the third chapter, I choose material that seems to me to exemplify the various types of possession I am discussing: songs which deal with embodiment and physicality; songs with religious or ritual connotations; songs by other artists of which Simone convincingly takes ownership; live performances that show the artist as servant and owner of her material. In considering lateness and the late voice, I select performances that deal with aspects of time, experience, memory and nostalgia. Fewer examples are discussed in the shorter chapter on Simone's legacy; that chapter, like this introduction, zooms out from specific analysis for the most part in order to place Simone in a wider context.

As will be clear from some of the qualifiers I have already employed, the choice of which material to discuss is, to a great extent, a subjective one. I have chosen recordings which speak strongly to me and, because they speak strongly to me, I have often devoted a considerable amount of space to them. This reduces the amount of material that can be discussed but I hope it also gives the book a depth which a more list-like survey would lack. At the same time, I have expanded the scope of the repertoire routinely discussed by considering material from each decade of Simone's recording career. While subjectivity is undoubtedly operating in the choice of material, I have also included discussions of many tracks which would be expected from any Nina Simone book, obvious examples being the songs 'Mississippi Goddam' and 'Four Women'. There are also many tracks which I consider classic or important in some way but which, in the final cut, had to be left out for reasons of space or fit. Discussion of these, and of songs still emerging into the light from dusty archives, will have to wait for another day.

1 Categories

Introduction: Eunice Waymon

Nina Simone was born Eunice Waymon in 1933 in the town of Tryon, North Carolina. Her mother, Mary Kate, was a Methodist minister and the religious lynchpin around whom much of Eunice's childhood experiences would form. Eunice's father, John Divine Waymon, had been a travelling entertainer in his youth but had settled down following his marriage to Mary Kate and worked as a barber and manager of a dry cleaning business. By the time of Eunice's birth, times were tough for the family, and money was much harder to come by during her early years. Eunice Waymon turned out to be a musical prodigy, able to play the family organ by the age of two and a half years and, by the time she was six, she was playing gospel music and hymns on the piano in her mother's church. Eunice's talents at the keyboard encouraged her parents to invest in private tuition and later convinced the local community to raise funds to have the child taught by a local English piano teacher called Muriel Massinovitch, known to Eunice as 'Miz Mazzy'. Miz Mazzy's work was continued by Eunice's high school teacher, Joyce Carroll. Eunice graduated with excellent grades from the private Allen High and earned herself a scholarship to study at Juilliard School of Music in New York. This opportunity, valuable as it was, was seen by her mother and Miz Mazzy as a precursor to auditioning for a place at the prestigious Curtis Institute of Music in Philadelphia. Eunice auditioned at Curtis in 1951 but was rejected. The reason given by the Institute was that, while highly gifted, she was outshone by other candidates; the reason that Nina Simone would continue to believe for the rest of her life was that she was refused because of her race.

During this time, Eunice had been offering piano lessons in New York to aspiring singers and dancers, a job which required her to expand her knowledge of contemporary popular music. Upon discovering that some of her students were making a better living than she was by performing in nightclubs, Eunice decided to try her luck as a performer, securing work in Atlantic City, New Jersey, and later in Philadelphia. If this represented one important step in changing her career aspirations, another came almost immediately when she turned to singing on the insistence of the manager of the Midtown Bar, the Atlantic City venue where she made her debut. Having turned to playing "the devil's music", Eunice Waymon took another decisive step by changing her name in order to prevent her religious mother learning of her new profession. She settled on "Nina Simone" by combining the Spanish word for "girl" (an endearment she had learned from a Spanish-speaking boyfriend – at least, this was one of the versions of the story she gave) and the name of the French actress Simone Signoret. Despite the name change and her experience at Curtis, Simone was still intent on a career as a classical musician and continued her lessons. Gradually, though, the nightclub work took over as her audience grew, drawn to the innovative way in which she presented a mixture of jazz, blues, folk and popular music alongside classically styled instrumental exercises and film and show tunes. Although it seems highly likely that Simone would have succeeded as a professional popular musician had her approach been less unusual, it is also probable that the very strategies she used to accommodate herself to popular music – adding Bach-influenced improvisations to songs and performing as if she were on a classical concert stage – were what helped to rapidly enlarge her audience.

Simone's debut at the Midtown occurred midway through 1954. For the next three years she circulated between Atlantic City, Philadelphia and New York, gaining an ever growing audience and attracting the ears of concert promoters and, eventually, record producers. Her official recording debut took place in late 1959 for the independent Bethlehem label in New York and Simone enjoyed her first recorded success when her version of the Gershwin classic 'I Loves You, Porgy' proved popular with radio audiences. In 1959 Simone settled in New York on a more permanent basis, becoming a fixture of the Greenwich Village art scene.

Nina Simone as "a Symptom of History"

The events outlined above are described in most accounts of Nina Simone's career and performances; many of these accounts are drawn from Simone's autobiography (Simone and Cleary 2003), which, as mentioned in the Introduction, is both an invaluable insight into the artist's life and another performance by Simone, with all the potential for mutation, revision and versioning that is the hallmark of her classic performances. The brief biographical narrative is included here, along with the comments about Simone's late career provided in the Introduction, both as a necessary contextualization of the artist and as a way of setting up the "evental" backdrop to many of the performances to be discussed in these chapters.

An event, as outlined briefly in the Introduction, can be considered both as something that occurs at a specific time and place and as an ongoing process, one that Alain Badiou (2005) defines as "fidelity to the event". In starting to link together aspects of Nina Simone's biography and autobiography with wider cultural and historical factors, I wish to keep both notions of event in play. The first specific event I want to highlight concerns a traumatic experience Eunice Waymon underwent at the age of eleven during a public piano recital:

> When I was eleven years old I was asked to give a recital in the town hall. I sat at the piano with my trained elegance while a white man introduced me, and when I looked up my parents, who were dressed in their best, were being thrown out of their front row seats in favour of a white family I had never seen before. And Daddy and Momma were allowing themselves to be moved. Nobody else said anything, but I wasn't going to see them treated like that and stood up in my starched dress and said if anyone expected to hear me play then they'd better make sure that my family was sitting right there in the front row where I could see them, and to hell with poise and elegance. So they moved them back. But my parents were embarrassed and I saw some of the white folks laughing at me (Simone and Cleary 2003, 26).

This was a devastating event for a girl who had grown up relatively immune to the injustices of racism: "All of a sudden it seemed a different world, and nothing was easy anymore" (26). What Simone experienced at this stage of her life was the collapsing together of a personal trauma with a larger and longstanding public, or cultural, trauma, namely the legacy of slavery that had left a permanent scar on the body of American society.

Ron Eyerman speaks of the trauma of slavery as "collective memory, a form of remembrance that grounded the identity-formation of a people". In addition to the brutal reality of those who lived and died in captivity, "slavery was traumatic in retrospect, and formed a 'primal scene' which could, potentially, unite all 'African Americans' in the United States, whether or not they had themselves been slaves or had any knowledge of or feeling for Africa"

(2001, 1). Eyerman distinguishes what he calls "cultural trauma" from individual, psychological trauma by emphasizing shared experience and inherited knowledge. The knowledge of trauma faced by one's ancestors is as important here as directly experienced events: "While it may be necessary to establish some event as the significant 'cause,' its traumatic meaning must be established and accepted, a process which requires time, as well as mediation and representation" (2).

Witnessing the treatment of others is also important here; Orlando Patterson, for example, notes that one of the features of a slave childhood "was the added psychological trauma of witnessing the daily degradation of [one's] parents at the hands of slaveholders" (1998, 40). The experience described by Patterson can be compared to the traumatic experience of the eleven-year-old Eunice Waymon at the piano recital. Simone, in remembering nearly fifty years later, even uses a metaphor that is chillingly reminiscent of slavery and post-Reconstruction racism: "The day after the recital I walked around feeling as if I had been flayed and every slight, real or imagined, cut me raw." In her memory Simone could still project defiant rage and an awareness of a developing identity to that moment: "But the skin grew back again a little tougher, a little less innocent, and a little more black" (Simone and Cleary 2003, 26–7). In her memory the individual and collective experiences, hers and those of her slave ancestors, have merged together. It is in the act of remembering, as Cathy Caruth points out, that the traumatic effect is produced, rather than during the original event: "To be traumatized is precisely to be possessed by an image or event" (1995, 4). Caruth follows Freud's emphasis on deferred action in her theorization of post-traumatic stress disorder. The traumatic dream for Freud is "the literal return of the event against the will of the one it inhabits". Traumatic dreams are often literal and non-symbolic: "It is this literality and its insistent return which thus constitutes trauma and points towards its enigmatic core: the delay or incompletion in knowing, or even in seeing, an overwhelming occurrence that then remains, in its insistent return, absolutely *true* to the event" (5, original emphasis). Trauma, to put it in terms derived from Badiou, shows fidelity to the event.

Eyerman's and Caruth's accounts both emphasize the structure of time which links the traumatic event irrevocably with history; in Caruth's words, post-traumatic stress disorder "is not a pathology . . . of falsehood or displacement of meaning, but of history itself . . . not so much a symptom of the unconscious, as it is a symptom of history" (1995, 5). This provides a useful way of navigating between those aspects of trauma associated with the personal and those considered via collective experiences; as history applies itself both to the individual and the society, so trauma ravages the individual body and the body politic.

Another crucial event in Simone's life was her rejection by the prestigious Curtis Institute in Philadelphia, where she had hoped to continue her music education. Although she had begun her musical career in the church, the music she really wished to play was Bach, Czerny and Liszt, wherein she "found a happiness I didn't have to share with anybody" (Simone and Cleary 2003, 51). At the time of her rejection by Curtis, Simone was still intending to spend her life playing such music. Having invested so much in her ambition and having had others invest so much in her, Simone had allowed herself to become subject to an act of faith, in this case not religious faith but the faith that music – classical music – would be her future. Instead, despite the great success she went on to achieve, the faith she had in music would be equally tempered with rejection and disavowal: in many ways, rejection was to become the trauma of her life. Simone remained bitter about the Curtis Institute in her later years, finding in it a painful example of American racism. In her autobiography she is explicit about her disappointment, providing a conflation of the past anger she wishes to represent and the present, residual anger of the moment of representation. She is similarly vocal about the incident in one of the interviews included in the 1992 documentary film *La Légende*. The film closes with a fantasy sequence in which Simone is seen playing Tchaikovsky's *Romeo and Juliet* with members of the Orchestre de Paris to an audience seated in a French formal garden and comprising Simone's daughter and a prominently positioned black couple, presumably representing her parents. Along with the music we hear the elderly Mrs Waymon giving her account of her daughter's traumatic childhood recital. Meanwhile we witness Simone's youthful ambitions seemingly realized as she returns to "real music".

The events highlighted above are vivid examples of the racially segregated world into which Simone was born and grew up, as well as being constitutive factors in the direction Simone's musical career would take. While the town hall recital would form a precursor to Simone's subsequent relationships with audiences, the Curtis rejection was both a signal of failure (the first time Simone had been told she was not musically gifted *enough*) and a determining moment in her future success as a popular musician. Simone's development as a popular musician exemplified a common experience for African American musicians in which social categorization was reflected in musical categorization. As Ingrid Monson emphasizes, "Segregation . . . concentrated a great deal of African American musical talent in the 'racially expected' genres of jazz, blues, and gospel since opportunities in other genres, such as classical music, were limited" (2007, 7). The "structural role" of social segregation is also highlighted in Nadine Cohodas's observation that, the specifics of Simone's rejection by the Curtis Institute aside, the whole process took place in a society in which racism continually disenfranchised certain groups: "If racism was indeed at play, it had shaped Eunice's chances long before she sat down to audition in one of Curtis's elegant mansions. Her competition had better and more training simply because they were white" (2010, 55). Ultimately, while the blurriness brought on by historical distance and the insidious and often unconscious ways in which prejudice operates mean that we are unlikely ever to know whether Simone was rejected by Curtis because of her colour, this gap in empirical knowledge in no way diminishes the very real impact that the rejection had on the artist throughout her subsequent career.

If Simone's autobiographical comments tended towards an emphasis on the evental, decisive moments in her life, this retroactive positing of eventness, with all its potential for misremembering, revision and myth-making, by no means invalidates the realness of the events. In fact, as will be suggested at various points in this book, a conception of memory as motivated act rather than accurate portrayal of events is arguably more useful in bringing together the life and work of an artist such as Simone. To say this is not to say that facts are unimportant, but rather to recognize the strategic importance of playing history and myth against each other, of recognizing the articulation of history as, in Walter Benjamin's words, "appropriating a memory as it flashes up in a moment of danger" (2006, 391). We can see this tension played out in the biographies of Nina Simone that have appeared in recent years. When placed against the diligent research and sober narration of Simone's most careful biographer to date, Nadine Cohodas, the biography by David Brun-Lambert (2009) is likely to strike many readers as brash, impertinent and opportunistic. Yet, Brun-Lambert's narrative is one that fits the perspective of Simone-as-event very effectively through its use of epic style, action, reaction and "evental" language. To take one example, we have already seen how Cohodas reflects on Simone's rejection by the Curtis

Institute. In contrast, Brun-Lambert treats the event with a significance that reflects Simone's own strategic use:

> At twenty, determined to become the first African-American classical concert performer in a still overtly segregationist country, she was rejected by the white jury from a music school. We could say that Eunice Waymon . . . died on that day, along with her dreams. But her anger never did – it persisted, swelled, grew, until another creature entirely came into being, belligerent, charismatic, resolute, gifted: Nina Simone. An artist with a mission (Brun-Lambert 2009, 1–2).

We know that Waymon/Simone would not have been the first African-American "classical concert performer", that Eunice did not die and that the process by which Eunice became Nina was far more complicated than is here suggested. However, there is still a powerful sense of truth, affirmation and faith in Brun-Lambert's refashioning of the tale, a sense of the importance of the event in the creation of subjectivity.

Little Girl Blue

Regardless of how we choose to narrate Nina Simone's story, there can be little doubt that the trauma she inherited and experienced was a direct result of categorization. It is important to consider the ways in which she was categorized due to her race and gender alongside the challenges she posed regarding musical categorization. The latter can be seen as a result of the former but also as an attempt to break free, which Simone did as she dismantled the barriers between styles, genres, norms and expectations. We need to be aware of this connection between racial and musical categorization early in our discussion of Simone's work because these events came early in her life, leading her towards the path she took (professionally and politically) and also because racial classification preceded and shaped the industry in which she forged her career.

Simone's defiance of musical categorization can be witnessed on her very first official recordings. Although these date from late 1957, the eleven selections that made up her debut album *Little Girl Blue* were not released until at least a year later.[1] By the time Simone came to record for Bethlehem, she had been honing her craft in bars and nightclubs for some time and, while her rejection by the Curtis Institute did not singlehandedly dissuade her from her ambitions to be a classical musician, it certainly focused her mind on what she was doing successfully, namely serving up a wildly mixed menu of classical, jazz, folk, pop and other sounds for nightclub patrons in search of something different. It made sense, therefore, to keep to this formula and style for her first official recordings and made her debut album "another irreversible step toward a pop career" (Cohodas 2010, 82). The mix of styles employed by Simone was a feature that many commentators immediately highlighted. When *Little Girl Blue* was released, the accompanying liner notes by Joseph Muranyi described Simone as "an unlikely combination of Marian Anderson and Ma Rainey", making reference to the African American classical singer and the early twentieth-century blues singer (B12, liner notes). Despite noting this fusion, Muranyi seemed keen to establish Simone as a jazz artist rather than a pop star, signalling one of the ways that the politics of authenticity, then as now, required an other (in this case, what Muranyi referred to as "the 'pop' style") against which a definition of authentic artistry could be projected.

The opening track of the album would seem to attest to Muranyi's jazz identification as Simone performs a rendition of Duke Ellington's 'Mood Indigo' with a typical jazz trio (piano, bass, drums). At the same time, the choice of material is interesting in that Ellington, like Simone, frequently rejected the "jazz" tag. Of equal importance is the way in which, as Daphne Brooks points out, Simone turns Ellington's tempo "inside out" (2011, 176). Brooks finds in Simone's first official recordings ample evidence of "an artist who defied the center, ran circles in the margins, and wove together 'highbrow' and 'lowbrow' forms to create an off-beat repertoire" (176). That said, by following 'Mood Indigo' with two tracks associated with Peggy Lee and the vocal traditions of jazz and torch songs, Simone does seem to stay within the category of the jazz artist as defined by Muranyi, where "jazz" designates an alteration to (or a signifying on) "the 'pop' style".

This is further exemplified by the title track of the album, a song written by Richard Rodgers and Lorenz Hart for the 1935 musical *Jumbo*. 'Little Girl Blue' had previously been recorded by Ella Fitzgerald and Frank Sinatra and would subsequently be recorded by Doris Day, Janis Joplin and the Carpenters among others. Simone's version is singular in that she introduces the song by playing a handful of bars from the Christmas carol 'Good King Wenceslas', which are then used as a countermelody to the main song. On the version on the debut album, Simone begins with the "Wenceslas" melody, which she then starts to develop for a minute as she might with a Bach fugue. Just as the drama is building, she cuts the improvisation and launches into the first line of Rodgers and Hart's song: "Sit there and count your fingers . . .". She then offers a fragile reading of what is essentially a melancholy song, part comfort for a lovelorn orphan, part yearning for the thrill of new romance. At various points throughout the song the "Wenceslas" melody reappears and it is also used to bring the performance to a close. This interweaving of the two songs was maintained when Simone returned to 'Little Girl Blue' at subsequent points in her career and differently weighted versions can be witnessed on the 1965 album *Let It All Out* and the DVD *Live at Montreux 1976*.

The title track is also significant in that it was the tune Simone used to test the guitarist Al Shackman when it was first suggested he accompany her. Shackman would go on to work with Simone on numerous occasions over the course of her career and he can be heard on many of her recorded performances. In her memoir, Simone describes her astonishment at the way in which Shackman was able to follow what she was doing and even to anticipate where she might go. After the guitarist passed the 'Little Girl Blue' test with flying colours, the pair "played Bach-type fugues and inventions for hours, and all the way through we hardly dared look at each other for fear that the whole thing would come tumbling down" (Simone and Cleary 2003, 59).

Although Shackman was not able to be part of the Bethlehem sessions, it is precisely this sense of fragility that flickers through Simone's recording of 'Little Girl Blue', especially the moments in the song where she pauses on the most forlorn imagery: the girl left alone, the raindrops, the narrator's melancholic observation that "you might as well surrender", and, perhaps most movingly, the word "blue" that ends the song. There is a signal here, perhaps more than with any of her other recordings from this session, of what would be a recurring theme in Simone's work, the interruption of an often swinging, soulful or funky set with a fragile lament that seemed to contain the weight of years. As listeners with the whole of Nina Simone's recorded legacy at our disposal, it is difficult not to hear in 'Little Girl Blue' an early example of the singer's late voice, even a precursor to the title track of her last studio album, *A Single Woman*.

A similar fusion of styles is brought to Simone's reading of 'Love Me or Leave Me', a song strongly associated with Billie Holiday but which Simone makes her own by inserting a classical piano solo quite different to the type of extemporization expected of a jazz trio setting. In comparison to the album's title track, 'Love Me or Leave Me' is an uptempo, swinging tune, as is the song that follows it, 'My Baby Just Cares for Me'. The latter combines the swing of jazz with piano extensions that, again, remain closer to classical styles than jazz. The instrumental 'Good Bait' forges a similar fusion, albeit this time with a first half that is played as a blues and a second half that is closer to Beethoven (the track originally came from the jazz repertoire, having been written for Count Basie's band).

'My Baby Just Cares for Me' would go on to be Simone's most well-known song, not only from this era but arguably from her entire career. However, the song that was picked up for radio play shortly after the release of *Little Girl Blue* was her version of 'I Loves You, Porgy', another number indelibly associated with Billie Holiday. Even as that song became a hit, however, Simone was embarking on a new era in her recording career, having signed with the Colpix label. Starting with *The Amazing Nina Simone* in 1959, Colpix would release ten albums by the artist, of which the first eight (1959–1963) can be regarded as original albums while the final two are more cobbled-together affairs that reissue earlier material. In what follows I use these albums as a starting point for discussing issues of categorization, for all of them display Simone's trademark eclecticism. They also represent her involvement in the late 1950s and early 1960s New York music scene, especially that which formulated around Greenwich Village. This fascinating art world was one which embraced politics, artistic experimentation, multiculturalism and eclecticism. It was the ideal place for Simone to explore the dismantling of musical boundaries.

Categorization: The Colpix Years

A number of arguments have already been aired regarding the problems of categorization. However, in order to speak about the music itself, categorization provides a useful starting point, even if discussion of a particular performance leads us far from where we thought the generic parameters should lie. Indeed, it is these excessive moments that help us to focus on what we think a particular style or genre "is". To describe something as "not jazz" is to engage in as much definition work as to assert that something "is jazz".[2] With regard to Simone, as Ashley Kahn says, "it's still easier to describe what she is not than what she is" (B10, liner notes).

The following pages, structured according to generic and stylistic categories, are written from the perspective of an initial premise that would assume categorization as a possible and workable endeavour. Only by attempting to fit Simone's performance choices into a range of categories (classical, jazz, blues and so on) can we determine the extent to which she was, and remains, uncategorizable. The process also allows us, by focusing mainly on the recordings Simone made for Colpix, to appreciate how the artist was multi-voiced from early in her career, reflecting and redefining inherited and existent musical styles and categories.

Classical and Jazz

Simone described her music at various times as "black classical music", a term which is both resonant in its seeming rightness and yet difficult to attach to any particular sound or style. What would black classical music be exactly? The adaptation of spirituals as found in the concerts of Paul Robeson? The music made by black artists such as Marian Anderson who worked in the bourgeois milieu of classical music? Or perhaps jazz music itself, which many have argued should be heard as America's own classical music? In an interview for *La Légende*, Simone defined "black classical music" as "an infusion of pop, gospel, classical, jazz, folk and ballads". While this definition may lack precision, one strategic reason for wanting to use the term "black classical" was no doubt the continuing anger Simone felt regarding the failure of her dream to become a classical pianist. Although she would not have been, as she sometimes claimed, the first classically trained black American concert pianist, nor the first African American woman to carve out a career in that white-dominated milieu, it is important to recognize Simone's determination to show her capabilities. The airs and graces she would occasionally assume, as much as her virtuosity at the keyboard, can be seen as markers of this desire to prove the refined power of black classical music.

One defining aspect of black classical music would be the type of fusion between jazz and classical styles that Simone had been developing from her time as a nightclub performer in Atlantic City, and which she essayed on her first album. The style that Simone developed at the Midtown, while working through the difficult decision to transfer from classical to popular styles, was showcased on the Colpix albums, many of which featured the artist in a live setting. Her fifth album for the label, *Nina Simone at the Village Gate* (1962), contains a fine example of Simone's classically flavoured style in her rendition of the 1920s Tin Pan Alley standard 'Bye Bye Blackbird' (B5, track 4). The version recorded by Simone and her band is an instrumental one; shorn of the familiar lyrics, the resulting performance showcases instrumental virtuosity, in particular the musical alchemy between Simone and Shackman. Simone's piano introduction is restrained and elegant, initially offering few clues to the identity of the song, then allowing fragments of the melody to enter. After nearly two minutes, Simone shifts to comping at the piano as if for a standard jazz rendition of 'Bye Bye Blackbird' and Shackman assumes the spotlight, the growing dynamism of his guitar work amplified and underlined by Bobby Hamilton's drum fills. At 3:32 Simone asserts her leadership via an insistently repeated note that pecks at the "Blackbird" melody before developing first into a jazz solo, then alternating scattered jazz notes with waves of tones and scales more associated with the teleology of classical style. Yet, even as she channels the techniques of European virtuosi from Bach to Liszt, the addition, at the six-minute mark, of wordless, scatted vocals, "blackens" the music, claiming it for a jazz-singing tradition that leads from Louis Armstrong to Abbey Lincoln and beyond. To use a less explicit term (though its use is no less resonant in its racial implications), we could follow Farah Jasmine Griffin and Salim Washington in their description of the way Billie Holiday "blued" the material she performed (Griffin 2001, 30, 203).

This description of 'Bye Bye Blackbird' runs the risk of suggesting that there are clear points when Simone switches from one style (jazz) to another (classical). For the purposes of analysis, of course, it is necessary to identify decisive, illustrative moments in the recording. Analysis requires at least the fantasy of stasis, of moments frozen long enough for interpretation to take place. Music, however, is a flowing, temporal experience and, while its temporal qualities do not make it resistant to analysis, we must remain alive to the ways in which various elements coalesce, mutate, relate, respond to, reflect and feed each other. The processes of "blackening" or "blueing" suggest ways by which we can recognize such flow in Simone's work. The interlacing, or overlaying, of the scatted vocal with classical piano style on 'Bye Bye Blackbird' highlights the extent to which we should stay alive to the hybridizing processes of musical performance even as we apply our attention to particular musical objects. Such processes are often recognized in discourse about music, for example when artists are described as "jazzing" or "jazzing up" pieces of music not previously associated with the genre of jazz.

Nina Simone's work invites us to see classical music as a process too, to note the inclusion into popular songs of certain signifiers of classical style (certain types of motivic figures, certain conventions, sections which are not "jazzed", which stay close to "the rules"). Describing the music of Chicago, in his poem "The Windy City", Carl Sandburg used the memorable phrase "they jazz the classics"; perhaps we could see Simone's contribution to black classical music as a determination to "classicalize" jazz.

The above description of "jazzing", "blacking" and "blueing" music should also be connected to the much-discussed concept of "Signifyin(g)", especially as utilized by Henry Louis Gates (1988) for African-American literature and Samuel Floyd (1995) for African-American music. As Floyd argues, Gates's theory of signifyin(g), in which formal processes (generally those of the dominant or hegemonic culture) are undermined, critiqued and played with by vernacular practices belonging to other traditions (in this case, those derived from Africa), allows a useful way of considering black music processes such as jazz. Jazz improvisations can thus be seen as "toasts – metaphoric renditions of the troping and Signifyin(g) strategies of African-American oral toasts". This process of "troping" is defined as "the transformation of preexisting musical material by trifling with it, teasing it, or censuring it" (1995, 8).

As with many musical labels or categories, jazz signals both a style and a process. The foregoing references to jazz have made use of both significations, emphasizing style where it was strategic to distinguish jazz from pop or classical, highlighting process when the act of "jazzing" was deemed of greater importance. Although a particular style may well come to be associated with a song once it is well known, it is important to remember that songs do not necessarily have inherent styles. Whenever a song is adapted to a style, done in a particular way, its feasibility and flexibility are tested and demonstrated. This does not mean that all songs can be adapted to all styles, or that some songs do not sound somehow truer when performed in a particular style. Bearing in mind these qualifications, songs still provide useful points of comparison as seemingly stable texts upon which to extemporize and innovate. The popularity of the "standard" in jazz relies upon the fact that there is at least the idea of an original, or standardized, template (a "classic", as Sandburg would put it) upon which to build new versions. The various processes involved in "jazzing the classics" – from Duke Ellington's lengthy suites, Miles Davis's cool phrasing and John Coltrane's sheets of sound to the versioning of the American songbooks undertaken by Ella Fitzgerald,

Sarah Vaughan and Dinah Washington – rapidly and extensively expanded the understanding of what it was possible to do with music and provided ample reason for considering jazz as one of the USA's greatest contributions to modernist art. This recognition did not, however, deliver jazz's innovators from the negative implications of racial categorization. Ingrid Monson identifies the paradoxical situation jazz found itself in as regards its status as a modern (and modernist) art form:

> The interest that both European and American modernist composers showed in jazz in the 1920s and 1930s, as well as the tendency of European audiences to recognize the "art" in jazz and to treat its musicians accordingly, encouraged many jazz musicians to think of themselves as artists in a high bohemian art sense. The conditions in the music industry under which they labored, however, were decidedly those of music for popular entertainment, with all of the racial stratifications of the early to mid-twentieth century intact (2007, 17–18).

It is clear from numerous comments made by Nina Simone throughout her career that she perceived – and wanted her audience to perceive – her music not only as art, but as art free from classification. In this she was not alone, for most, if not all, of the musicians mentioned above made similar comments.

Amongst those closest to Simone in their stylistic attempts at escaping classification were her precursors Hazel Scott and Kitty White. Scott (1920–1981) was a black Trinidadian-American pianist who combined classical and jazz styles, providing a template for the kind of music Simone would play. Her 1955 trio recordings with Charles Mingus and Max Roach (C30) provide an interesting comparison to Simone's work, with Scott veering between jazz traditions and Bach-influenced extemporization. In the 1940s Scott had been a regular performer at Café Society, the nightclubs operated by Barney Josephson in New York City which showcased progressive (and often highly politicized) African American music. Scott was involved in a series of concerts put on by the club entitled "From Bach to Boogie-Woogie" and, during the 1940s, she recorded a landmark series of discs that incorporated elements of classical, boogie-woogie and jazz. Simone reportedly held Scott in awe, having pictures of the artist covering one of her walls at Allen High (Cohodas

2010, 43) and the two would later become friends.[3] Kitty White (1923–2009) worked as a nightclub singer (and initially pianist) on the West Coast of the USA and recorded a series of albums between the mid-1950s and mid-1960s that could, again, be heard as templates for Simone's art. Where Hazel Scott had provided a model for the combination of jazz and classical music, White could be seen as influential in terms of her eclectic source material, combining jazz, blues, folk and international music styles with film and show tunes in a manner that seemingly defied categorization. In her autobiography, Simone reported that she learned the song 'Plain Gold Ring' from White. She may well have been referring to White's album *Cold Fire!* (1956 [C39]), which also included a version of another Simone favourite, 'The Other Woman'. While *Cold Fire!* found White primarily adopting styles that would be classed as jazz, her contemporaneous collection *Folk Songs* (C39) presented a range of songs often associated with white folk and country performers, sung in a manner not unlike the black folk singer Odetta.

Scott, White and Simone all provide fascinating stories of musical eclecticism, yet all three were and remain classified as jazz singers, at least as far as record companies and retailers are concerned. Simone, the most famous of the trio, is generally included in jazz sections of record shops but excluded from jazz reference books and academic jazz studies. The approach is inconsistent, however. Will Friedwald, for example, grants her only a couple of dismissive references in his 1992 book *Jazz Singing*, yet provides a substantial section on the artist in his more recent *Biographical Guide to the Great Jazz and Pop Singers*, claiming that "in 1959, practically everything she did could be considered jazz" (2010, 414). The change in attitude may well be a reflection of a more general notion of what now passes as jazz singing, with Simone seen as a pioneer of an eclectic style that has become much more the norm in the twenty-first century. As Friedwald suggests, Simone's style casts a shadow over contemporary singers such as Diana Reeves and Cassandra Wilson. The producers of the Naxos "Jazz Icons" series of DVDs, meanwhile, felt it necessary in 2008 to include a lengthy note justifying the inclusion of Nina Simone in the series. Having polled their customer base during the production of the second series of discs in 2007 and received polarized opinions, the team decided not to include Simone, only to reverse their "final decision" for the third series.

Blues

There have been a number of debates during the course of blues history about women's involvement in the music. While many early blues historians were quick to assert the places of the "classic blues queens" such as Ma Rainey, Bessie Smith, Clara Smith, Ethel Waters, Alberta Hunter and Ida Cox, some also engaged, whether intentionally or not, in a process of authenticating certain strands of blues more associated with male performers by making a distinction between "commercial" styles, such as those in which the blues queens participated, and non-commercial, traditional or roots styles such as the country blues. Recognizing that such distinctions perpetuated gender-biased narratives that denied active female involvement in vernacular culture, subsequent feminist scholars sought to highlight the personal, professional and sexual – in short, political – freedom enjoyed by the early blues queens, who were able to transgress the roles expected of their race, gender and class (Carby 1998; Davis 1998; P. Collins 2009). While this work offered a series of crucial interventions, it did little to alter the perception of black women as primarily singers of the blues. More recent work has thus attempted to increase awareness of the wide variety of musics in which black women have been involved (Hayes and Williams 2007).

When speaking of Nina Simone's connection to the blues, many commentators refer to the names of early blues queens such as Ma Rainey and Bessie Smith. When Simone performed the blues, she certainly adopted something of the style of these women. To hear her sing 'Trouble in Mind', 'I Want a Little Sugar in My Bowl' or 'Chauffeur' is to recognize the inheritance of Rainey and Smith. At the same time, Simone was more eclectic than these singers; in thinking of her as a blues musician, then, it is necessary to consider both the stylistic features of the music she performed and the way in which she inherited aspects of the black feminism that Angela Davis and Hazel Carby see as the legacy of the blues queens.

As mentioned above, songs do not necessarily denote particular styles. Blues music, however, has tended to be associated with particular structures and particular types of repetition. So it is understandable that the liner notes to Simone's album to *At Newport* should describe 'Trouble in Mind' as a blues, given that, Simone's use of the piano aside, her version of the song could be stylistically placed alongside those of Lightnin' Hopkins and Mance Lipscomb (B3). But what about when we hear Roscoe Holcomb sing it? Does it become folk music because Holcomb is associated with "old-time" Appalachian styles and was a key inspiration for the post-war American Folk Revival? A similar point can be made with reference to 'House of the Rising Sun', which Simone recorded on *At the Village Gate* and again on *Sings the Blues*. The song is often considered a folk song (and Simone introduces it as such on the *Village Gate* recording) but, like 'Trouble in Mind', it features elements that lend themselves well to blues renditions. Alan Lomax collected versions of the song entitled 'The Rising Sun Blues' in 1937, while Roscoe Holcomb's version (entitled 'House in New Orleans') is, as far as "sound, style and feeling" go, akin to the blues (Cohen in C20, liner notes). Material such as this was no doubt part of the "common stock" of interracial music that still existed in the rural south in the early decades of the twentieth century (Russell 2001). Versions of 'House of the Rising Sun' by Lead Belly and Josh White emphasized the blues elements of the song through the use of vocal inflection (Lead Belly) or guitar licks (White). Both versions were no doubt influential on Simone's Greenwich Village contemporaries Dave Van Ronk and Bob Dylan (who both performed the song), and may well have influenced her own reading. On the earlier live recording, Al Shackman backs Simone with the kind of guitar licks and slides that had "blued" Josh White's 1947 version, while Simone's vocal combines the stately pace of Billie Holiday, the exploration of the note associated with jazz singing (for example, the Holiday-like "ne-eds" at 2:14), or the interjections and hollers of the blues or gospel singer ("Lord" at 2:35, "Somebody go get my baby sister", 2:44–2:50 [B5]).

An important aspect to note about the blues is the way that style interacts with feeling. Blues as feeling may prompt descriptions of sadness, lowdown states, fatalism and passivity, but such descriptions fail to note the transcendent qualities of singing and playing. As Kevin Young writes,

> With the blues, the form fights the feeling. Survival and loss, sin and regret, boats and heartbreak, leaving and loving, a pigfoot and a bottle of beer – the blues are a series of reversals, of finding love and losing it, of wanting to see yourself dead in the depths of despair, and then soon as the train comes down the track, yanking your fool head back (Young 2003, 11–12).

'House of the Rising Sun' bears this out; for all its desperation and blues feeling, it still offers, as a musical text, a hope of redemption. As mentioned below, Simone's revisiting of the song in 1967 would make this more explicit.

In addition to those songs from Simone's Colpix repertoire that could be identified as blues, it is worth highlighting two albums for subsequent record labels that were explicitly designed and marketed as blues records. The first of these was *Pastel Blues*, an album released by Philips in 1966 (B10, disc 2). The album's opening song, 'Be My Husband', utilizes a "chain gang" style in its percussive technique, aligning to styles occasionally adopted by Lead Belly and, later, Odetta and to 'Work Song', the Nat Adderley instrumental to which Oscar Brown Jr. added words and which Simone performed. The technique, enhanced by the way in which Simone highlights the rhythm as much as the melody of the song, suggests the domesticity pleaded for in the lyric may in fact be imprisoning, presumably not what the song's writer (Simone's then-husband, Andy Stroud) had intended. Simone's voice swoops to non-verbal vocal sounds between the lines of the song, referencing connections between the country blues and African precursors. 'Nobody Knows You When You're Down and Out' reprises a blues performed earlier by Simone on the Ellington tribute. It is a fairly standard piano-based blues, no doubt learned from the recordings of Bessie Smith, and foregoes the brass used on the earlier version in favour of a gradually strengthening vocal played out over the keyboard lines. 'Trouble in Mind' is another track reprised from the Colpix era and uses classic blues piano licks doubled by guitar fills between each line. 'Tell Me More' initially represents a more abstract piano piece, suggesting Thelonius Monk with vocals, though a blues harp adds an appropriately bluesy texture. 'Chilly Winds Don't Blow', a song previously recorded by Simone in a rather different form for Colpix, is given a blues reading (with much emphasis on the repeated "A" lines of each verse and interjections of "oh baby" and "my baby" as between-line punctuation) but retains its gospel-derived message of hope and yearning. 'Ain't No Use' follows a similar piano-blues path, Simone using a vocal style that would later come to be identified with soul as much as blues; about two minutes in, however, the piano ventures into the realm of classical style, a reminder that Simone was rarely content to keep things simple, at least at keyboard level. The other tracks on the album are 'End of the Line', closer to the show tunes and torch songs with which Simone had been identified early in her career, the Billie Holiday classic 'Strange Fruit' (discussed in the next chapter) and the ten-minute, virtuosic gospel number 'Sinnerman' (discussed below).

By the following year, Simone had moved to the RCA label and her first release for them was *Nina Simone Sings the Blues*. That album presented the artist in a then-conventional blues setting, with guitar and bass providing stylistically recognizable lines, the electric lead adding licks between the lines and blues harp giving additional texture. Simone's vocal veered between the shouting style of Bessie Smith ('Do I Move You') and a smoother, more pop-orientated, or beat group, direction ('Day and Night'). 'I Want a Little Sugar in My Bowl' derived from Bessie Smith and used the classic blues queen's double entendres to offer a bawdy and seductive message supported by a smooching saxophone (a relatively rare sound in Simone's recordings). Perhaps the most startling track on the album was 'Backlash Blues', with words by Langston Hughes. Unlike the other blues, which referred to timeless themes of love and loss, this was an obviously contemporary number, making specific reference to the Vietnam War and to the continuing mistreatment of people of colour in the USA. As discussed in the next chapter, Simone was, by the time of this album, explicitly confronting issues of civil rights in her concerts, interviews and recordings. 'Backlash Blues', a visceral, electric blues, contributes to this by connecting contemporary concerns of the 1960s with a longstanding African American protest style, smuggling a message of subversion into the by-then familiar vehicle of the urban blues.

Again there were exceptions to the blues style. Gospel was also represented by 'Real Real', while gospel and soul seem to be the driving forces behind Simone's reprise of 'House of the Rising Sun', with its surprisingly bright tempo, its shout-singing and unmistakable groove. In stark contrast to earlier renditions (including those of Bob Dylan, Dave Van Ronk, the Animals and Simone herself), this is the song of an unrepentant sinner, a cousin of Bessie Smith and Ma Rainey. 'My Man's Gone Now', a song from *Porgy and Bess* known to audiences via smoky versions by Ella Fitzgerald, Sarah Vaughan and Julie London, represents the bluesier end of jazz rather than blues itself. Despite or because of these diversions, the closing track of the album, 'Blues for Mama', is a classic stop-start blues number which cements the feeling that *Nina Simone Sings the Blues* is, much like *Pastel Blues*, an appropriately titled collection of songs.

In addition to songs which might be defined as blues, we can also find in Simone's early repertoire a range of material infused with a more general "blueness". Songs such as 'Mood Indigo', 'Little Girl Blue' and 'Blue Prelude' absorb this blueness into other musical styles, some more closely related to the blues than others. By the mid-twentieth century, as Richard Williams notes, this blueness was all-pervasive in popular culture, especially music:

> Blue gardens. Blue valentines. Blue kisses, Blue velvet. Blue and sentimental. I'm blue. Love is blue. Way to blue. Blue on blue (heartache on heartache). A nice word to say – and to sing, with its explosive initial double-consonant immediately softened, then succeeded by a long and shapely vowel. Born to be blue. Midnight blue. Almost blue. Blue moon. Blue angel. Blue train. Blue notes, of course: the flattened thirds and sevenths of the blues. No colour has so saturated music over the last hundred years, while permitting so many shadings (2009, 37–8).

One way both the blues and a more general blueness had shaded popular music earlier in the century was through the vehicle of the torch song. Although torch singers were generally distinguished from blues singers through race, repertoire and recording milieu, there were a number of connections between them, not least in the seemingly fatalistic and (again, seemingly) defeatist nature of the song lyrics they sang (Moore 1989). The artist who most obviously represented blues and torch aspects was Billie Holiday, who incorporated a number of torch songs into her repertoire. The torch song, characterized as "a lament sung by a woman who desperately loves a commonplace or even brutish man" and "an elegy to unrequited or no longer requited love [without] the earthiness or playful eroticism of contemporary blues lyrics" (32), partakes of the kind of sentimentalism that Williams associates with blueness. In this it also shares something with country music and, as will be discussed in Chapter 4, it can be illuminating to consider performers like Holiday and Simone alongside "sentimental" country singers such as Hank Williams (another performer often drawn to blues styles and bluesy lyrics). Simone performed a number of songs that fit at least some of the above definitions of the torch song and the term has certainly been applied to her repertoire over the years. Examples would include 'He Needs Me' (from her debut album), 'That's Him Over There' (from *The Amazing*), 'You Can Have Him' (from *At Town Hall*), 'Keeper of the Flame' (from *High*

Priestess of Soul) and, to a certain extent, 'The Other Woman' (which Simone performed throughout her career). These and other songs echoed Simone's torch singer precursors, at times presenting, as Farah Jasmine Griffin notes of Billie Holiday, "the tragic, ever-suffering black woman singer who simply stands center stage and naturally sings of her woes" (Griffin 2001, 31). Griffin, of course, is keen to dispel the myth of Holiday as victim and rightly focuses on the artistic skill necessary to create that sense of naturalness. Perhaps there is not quite the same necessity when dealing with Simone, who was able to assert her strength and autonomy on enough occasions to overshadow the other instances in which she seemed to lose both.

The general sense of the blues found in torch songs and other types of popular song could be connected to a narrative that asserts that the blues was exploited and watered down in its transference to other popular styles. For Patricia Hill Collins, "commodification of the blues and its transformation into marketable crossover music have virtually stripped it of its close ties to African-American oral traditions" (Collins 2009, 122). Langston Hughes's poem 'Note on Commercial Theatre' (Hughes 1995, 215–6) lamented the stealing of "my blues" by Broadway shows but hoped that "someday, somebody'll / Stand up and talk about me" and "sing about me / And put on plays about me!" (all of which was borne out by Hughes himself and his friends Lorraine Hansberry and Nina Simone among others).

What such narratives occasionally fail to take into account is the extent to which blues, like other vernacular musics of the twentieth century, was engaged in what Richard Peterson (1998) calls "the dialectic of hard-core and soft-shell" from its inception. In other words, blues, like country music, was marked by issues of authenticity and commercialism from the moment it was recognized as a popular music. Blues was, as Marybeth Hamilton (2007) suggests, as much an invention of the phonographic era as it was an ongoing tradition. To highlight this is not to want to deny connections to earlier African American traditions, but rather to question the teleology of a narrative that moves from an originary or authentic past to a degraded, commercialized present. Neither does this deny or de-authenticate the vital political role that performers such as Bessie Smith and Ma Rainey were able to perform from within the "degraded" culture industry. It was their commercial attractiveness that allowed them to articulate the messages of freedom and struggle that theorists such as Davis and Collins have celebrated.

Gospel

Coming from a strict religious background, Simone had had experience of "church language" from an early age. In her memoir, she recounts how, as a young girl, she would play piano in church to accompany the gospel singing of the congregation. This gave her a sense of the power of performance: "When I played I could take a congregation where I wanted – calm them down or lift them up until they became completely lost in the music and atmosphere" (Simone and Cleary 2003, 19). She describes how people in church were seized by the music, finding themselves "transported" to another place. Meanwhile her mother referred to non-church music as "real" music, ordering her daughter not to "play any of those real songs" (16). While Eunice Waymon's decision to do just this would lead to the adoption of a new name and subsequent fame, the music of the church remained a strong feature in Nina Simone's repertoire.

The sacred and the secular have frequently been presented as twin strands in African American music over the past two centuries. As many scholars have noted, the boundaries between these supposed styles of music are always shifting and there are numerous examples of musicians who moved between the two worlds, from Thomas A. Dorsey to Sam Cooke and Aretha Franklin. However, that does not mean that the perception of the split was unimportant. For Nina Simone, the sacred/secular split, if it did figure, may have been just one more case of double consciousness, of being between two worlds, but it would appear from her memoir that there was some initial discomfort in negotiating her path between them, just as there was in her weaving between classical and popular styles. As for many performers before her, leaving the musical milieu of the church for the world of "real songs" was also a leave-taking from home and her past. In *La Légende* we witness Simone making a trip home to reunite with her mother and her daughter, during which she is filmed playing for the local church congregation as a kind of homecoming. On *Fodder on My Wings* (1982) – an album imbued with a sense of lateness and retrospection through its experiential perspective on Simone's life and career, her deceased father and a religious reconciliation of sorts – Simone introduced a version of the gospel song 'Heaven Belongs to You' (also known as 'If You Pray Right') by speaking about her father singing it when she was three and also calling it an "African song" (B8, track 10). The references to ancestral and cultural roots bear witness to some of the ways in which Simone returned to gospel throughout her career as a way of reconnecting with where she was from.

Gospel featured on the very earliest recordings Simone made for Colpix, with *The Amazing Nina Simone* containing 'Children Go Where I Send You' and 'Chilly Winds Don't Blow'. 'Children' utilizes a classic barrelhouse piano style that became associated with gospel following the pioneering work of Arizona Dranes, asserting a sense of joy in playing and, as Simone's commanding vocal enters, in singing too (B1, track 2). Backed by drums which match the piano riffs, Simone drives the vocal home, speeding up her delivery as the song progresses to impart a sense of drive and momentum, of being taken over by the spirit of the music and by the incantatory magic of the song lyric: "eight for the eight that stood at the gate / seven for the seven came down from Heaven / six for the six that couldn't get fixed", and so on to the inevitable climax of "one for the little bitty baby / who was born born born in Bethlehem". In fact, the final line is also one of the first because this song, like 'The Twelve Days of Christmas', starts with the one, then accumulates one number on each verse, providing a forward-reverse development and, ultimately, a cyclical structure as the song closes once again on "born in Bethlehem". Simone displays further mastery over her material by suddenly cutting the hectically paced, syllable-based delivery of the lyrics at the song's conclusion (2:17) to use melisma to double the syllable of "was" and extend the word "born" before the climactic "in Beth-le-he-em". Throughout this version, the vocal harmonies or responses we might expect from a gospel song are absent, with Simone's the only voice present. Other versions of the songs have included such harmonies. The Golden Gate Quartet, exponents of the "jubilee style" of gospel singing, used only vocal harmonies in their version of 'Go Where I Send Thee', which dates from the 1930s. The song was also incorporated into *Black Nativity*, a Broadway show written by Langston Hughes which used gospel numbers sung by Marion Williams and Alex Bradford and their respective groups. The *Black Nativity* version includes both the Dranes-style barrelhouse piano and the vocal harmonies of the gospel choir (D2, side 2, track 6).

If participation was only hinted at in the studio recording, Simone took the opportunity to work the song for all its improvisatory, participatory properties in live performance. At the 1961 Village Gate concert recorded by Colpix, she provided an extended rendition of the song (B5, track 11). Opening more or less as normal she then drawls an instruction to her band (Al Shackman on guitar, Chris White on bass and Bobby Hamilton on drums) in a deliberately Southern accent: "Take your time, boys, we've got a while to go now". Although Simone was born and grew up in the South, she had, by the time she began performing publically, removed many traces of a Southern accent from her speaking and singing. This was no doubt due to the training she received from Miz Mazzy and Allen High as she prepared to be a concert pianist. She would later mock such preparation in her protest song 'Mississippi Goddam' as being made "to talk real fine just like a lady" as a way of escaping stereotypes attached to southern, working-class black women. Whatever her reasons for adopting the commanding and relatively accent-free "queenly" voice she would be known for, Simone would frequently move into other voices as part of her performance style (particularly notable on her composition 'Four Women'). Her gospel voice should therefore be understood as one of a variety of vocal masks adopted by Simone; on the *Village Gate* version of 'Children', that voice is also regionalized, both via her instruction to her band members and by the way she asks the audience if they've ever been to a revival meeting, following up with "you're in one now!" The act is clearly an effective one because, following various extemporizations on the main "Children go where I send you" theme, an audience participation occurs in which the crowd clap along as though possessed. Listening in, we witness Simone's enjoyment in the power she has to transport her congregation, to "send" her children where she wishes.

When considering Simone as a singer of blues, folk, gospel and spirituals, it is important to keep an eye and ear open to the work of her contemporary, Odetta, who had been recording a mixture of all these types of music since the mid-1950s. Odetta was generally classified as a folk singer and seen to be continuing the lineage of Huddie Ledbetter (Lead Belly) and Woody Guthrie. It was not unusual for folk singers of the time to include gospel songs given the latter's origins in the spiritual and field song tradition, and Odetta included a number of songs associated with jubilee quartets in her repertoire. Interestingly, Odetta was a classically trained musician and her voice, especially in her early career, often evoked the power of the classical or opera singer – pure, ungrainy, unwavering from the melody – rather than the "natural", untrained style associated with early folk singers and later post-revival artists. Odetta's style, not unlike that of Paul Robeson and Joan Baez, can be seen to represent a moment where, partly through the concert venue conventions of the time and partly through a desire for absolute clarity in the communication of the lyric, folk singing verged on classical styles. 'Children Go Where I Send Thee' was part of Odetta's live show from early in her career. A 1954 recording from her show at the Tin Angel in San Francisco finds her performing the song on guitar and chanting the vocal in a style somewhere between the church and the opera stage (C28, track 15). Odetta's vocal power is clear but it is questionable to what extent an audience or congregation would be "transported" by her elegant rendition.[4]

While it could be argued that Simone presented her "folk" material in a fairly restrained manner, keeping something of the textual reverence displayed by Odetta, her gospel numbers tended to be wilder affairs, possessed of a different kind of power to that found in Odetta's voice. Power, pleading and confusion are the key markers in Simone's reading of 'Sinnerman', a track described by Richard Middleton as a "last-day drama" (2006, 122). Certainly, there is an apocalyptic feel to the song, aided by its epic running time (notable in at least three recorded versions by Simone[5]), its "implacable" piano vamp (122) and its depiction of an unredeemable sinner caught between God and the Devil. Over the endless, infectious piano, the song is played out in what initially seems like a duologue in which the speaking roles are limited to two voices, not necessarily in conversation. The Sinnerman is addressed as "you" at various points but speaks as "I" for most of the song, although it is not difficult to imagine, given the terror and confusion that reign over this transgressing subject, that everything we hear represents the Sinnerman's own bewildered thought and speech. As in 'The City of Refuge', a song recorded by the gospel-blues artist Blind Willie Johnson, the protagonist is constantly running. The relentless verses chase the sinner as he runs to the rock, to the sea and to the river (both of which are "bleeding" and "boiling"), each time finding neither refuge nor respite from his all-seeing, vengeful God. Even when he runs "to the Lord" he is told to "run to the Devil" and is left with little option but to plead with the Lord to "bring down power".

The power play of the text is matched by the shifting dynamics of the song. Eventually the implacable piano crashes to a halt (3:35) and drums, bass and guitar carry the groove. There is a clapping interlude with no instrumental accompaniment, during which the piano starts up again, slowly at first and then gradually building back into the vamp and a repeat of some of the verse elements – the boiling river and sea. Simone's voice rises to a shout ("where were you when you ought to be praying?") and, as the band move into a repeat of the "bring power" section, the pleading becomes desperate, eventually moving into a wordless kind of scat that Middleton describes as "glossolalic" (a reference to the religious practice of speaking in tongues), succeeded by "a drum-kit conclusion of Old Testament severity" (2009, 123). Like the sinner, we are caught between a rock and a hard place, not knowing where to go or what to expect. It is tempting to read the song as one of paranoia, or, at least, of the kind of double consciousness alluded to elsewhere in this book, a consciousness that offers the subject an always already confused sense of belonging. In a lesser known version of 'Sinnerman' included on the album *Gospel According to Nina Simone* (B16, track 15), the artist inserts a line from her signature song 'Mississippi Goddam' – "I don't belong here, I don't belong there" – which serves as both an intertextual reference for performer and audience and as a way of cementing the Sinnerman's predicament.

The gospel aspects of Simone's music can be connected to her classical music tastes via the space of the church; Bach, after all, is religious music as much as any backsliding number. The church keyboard is also a site of improvisation and a place from which one can start, stop, extend or extemporize as befits the necessity of the occasion. Via what we might call "the church of Nina Simone", the artist would come to treat the stage as the site from which she gave her sermons, acting as both organist and preacher. In a short feature made about Simone in 1970, she is shown performing Billy Taylor's gospel-like 'I Wish I Knew How It Would Feel To Be Free', during which she moves into an impromptu religious discourse. This footage is intercut with an interview in which Simone discusses revival meetings and describes how her performances are open-ended and variable.

Folk

While discussing the difficulty that critics had in categorizing her music, Simone claimed, "If I had to be called something it should have been a folk singer, because there was more folk and blues than jazz in my playing" (Simone and Cleary 2003, 69). While we have to treat Simone's self-categorizations with as much care as those of any other commentator, it is nonetheless worth considering her as a folk singer. As she suggests in her autobiography, one of the ways in which she was close to folk music and its audience was via her involvement in the Greenwich Village music scene and by the interest shown by (mainly white) folk music fans in blues music and musicians of the pre-World War II era.

In describing the time she spent performing in Greenwich Village, Simone highlights a growing desegregation in musical tastes and crowds:

> The folk kids were discovering blues players that the jazz people knew so well they regarded them as old history, nothing to do with what was happening; but to the white kids it was somebody else's history they were hearing, so it was new and exciting. And the jazz players had their ears and minds open to other influences – they had to, or else they wouldn't be able to play like they did (Simone and Cleary 2003, 68).

Some of the ways in which these worlds came together can be seen by considering the song 'Black Is the Color of My True Love's Hair', which Simone often performed during her early career. Often described in liner notes as a "Norwegian folk song", 'Black Is the Color . . .' had been part of the American folk repertoire for a considerable period before Simone offered her interpretation of it. It appears in Jean Ritchie's 1965 anthology *Folk Songs of the Southern Appalachians*, where it is listed as having been collected by Cecil Sharp in 1916 in North Carolina, Simone's home state (Ritchie 1997, 88). The song is often sung from the perspective of a man speaking of a woman, though Simone changes the personal pronouns in the version included on *At Town Hall* (1959 [B4, track 1]), a practice she would subsequently repeat when performing other writers' material. Whatever the provenance of the song, it could not have failed to have other identifications given the racial politics of the time, and a sense of identity assertion could be identified here that would find subsequent articulation in the more explicit 'Brown Baby', 'Four Women' and 'To Be Young, Gifted and Black'.

In addition to changing the pronouns of the song – a practice often avoided by folk singers who wish to show fidelity to the text rather than equate themselves with the protagonist of the lyric – Simone bases her version around a piano setting. While this is hardly surprising given that the piano was her instrument and that this performance was part of her first major New York concert, it does connect the performance to a longstanding classical music convention of incorporating folk songs into more "tasteful" or "artistic" styles and thus raises questions as to whether or not Simone would be considered a "folk singer" by the standards of the time, or indeed those of the present day. Still, the main feature of Simone's rendition is her voice, its warm tone hovering over the fairly muted piano chords (her keyboard virtuosity only emerges for brief spells between verses). Simone would offer a very similar reading of the song on her 1966 album *Wild Is the Wind*, by which time the association of folk music with stringed instruments was firmly established, as was a folk "style". Simone herself was not impervious to this folk style, as can be heard in her interpretation of Bob Dylan's 'Ballad of Hollis Brown' (on 1966's *Let It All Out*), where she is accompanied solely by driving acoustic guitar, the pounding rhythm adding a sense of doomed fatality to the song's tragic narrative.

'Black Is the Color . . .' has an interesting connection to classical and jazz music, having been used by both Luciano Berio and Patty Waters as the basis for longer works. The version of the song that Berio used in 1964 for his song cycle *Folk Songs* was one rewritten by John Jacob Niles, himself a fascinating character in the bringing together of classical and folk music. In late 1965, Patty Waters used the same version of the song that Simone had used as the basis for a 14-minute exploration of avant-garde vocal techniques on her album *Sings* (C38, track 8). Much of Waters's performance involves a violent interrogation of the word 'black', emphasizing the volatility of the term and encouraging a reading of the song in which black identity is foregrounded (Waters, a white singer, was operating in a musical milieu – free jazz – that would align itself strongly with the black power movement).

A "black pride" reading of the song would also seem to apply to the version which appears on Simone's album *Black Gold*, a live album recorded in 1969 (B7, disc 2, track 1). The album opens with the announcer, Ed Williams, quoting from Langston Hughes. A version of 'Black Is the Color . . .' follows, not significantly different to that featured on earlier albums. Having completed that version, the band perform a second version (ibid., track 2), which takes its lead from the acoustic guitar and utilizes a different, but complementary melody, a different vocalist (guitarist Emile Latimer) and singing style, different words and a different gender perspective. The first line of the song is the same, but then some changes are made: "black is her body, so firm, so bold / black is her beauty, her soul of gold". The subsequent narrative and instrumental style guide the song very closely to what would have been, at that time, a contemporary folk style, albeit with the blues/jazz tinge utilized by singers such as Fred Neil or Tim Buckley.

If analysis of a particular song has not necessarily brought us closer to determining Nina Simone as a folk artist, we might do better by considering her attitude and approach to music. She was a fine example of the "folk process" that would allow often radical changes to musical material while still maintaining strong links to tradition. As already noted, folk singers of the time (the time of the American Folk Revival, of which Simone was very much a part during her stay in Greenwich Village) would incorporate musical styles that went beyond a European-derived definition of "folk", incorporating music styles such as blues and gospel and also looking further afield to international folk styles.

Other Styles

The foregoing has centred discussion around some of the categories with which Simone was most commonly connected in the early part of her career: classical, jazz, blues, gospel and folk. While she was never marketed as a classical artist, her classical training was frequently alluded to and brought into dialogue with the vernacular styles under which her recordings were more explicitly presented. These categories are hopefully sufficient to provide an initial examination of Simone's music in terms of genre and style. Rather than catalogue the many other styles she explored, I bring this chapter to a close by considering Simone's last major albums for Colpix, *At Carnegie Hall* and *Folksy Nina*, both recorded live at Carnegie Hall in May 1963 (B2). Doing so will allow us to add at least two more categories to Simone's repertoire, namely international songs and songs associated with films and shows.

The Carnegie Hall concerts represented a major breakthrough for Simone, given the prestige of the venue and its association with classical music and with major names in jazz, folk and popular music. The venue had also played host to a number of performers who offered a similarly eclectic repertoire to Simone, Harry Belafonte and Pete Seeger having both released live albums recorded there. Belafonte's 1959 album (C3) was divided into three acts representing different "worlds": "Moods of the American Negro", including folk and blues classics such as 'Sylvie', 'Cotton Fields' and 'John Henry'; "In the Caribbean", covering some of the material with which Belafonte was most associated, such as 'Day O', 'Jamaica Farewell' and 'Mama Look A Boo Boo'; and "Round the World", featuring the Israeli song 'Hava Nageela', the Irish classic 'Danny Boy' and the Mexican love song 'Cu Cu Ru Cu Cu Paloma'. Seeger, meanwhile, included numerous examples of what would now be called "world music" in his 1963 sets: 'Lua Do Sertao' from Brazil; 'Polyushke Polye' from Russia; the Japan-themed 'Genbaku O Yurusumagi'; the Spanish

Civil War song 'Viva La Quince Brigada'; the South African freedom song 'Tshotsholosa'; and Seeger's signature 'Guantanamera' (*sic* passim [C32]).

Simone would bring a similar internationalism to her Colpix albums, drawing on African, Middle Eastern and European tunes in addition to the American vernacular styles with which she was already associated. Her Carnegie sets did not travel quite as extensively as earlier concerts but they still included Israeli songs, English folk songs and the theme music from the 1957 film *Sayonara* which drew on Japanese scales and, in Simone's performance, Japanese instrumental styles. If not thoroughly international, it nevertheless introduced an alternative sonority to the American concert hall. In addition to the *Sayonara* theme, Simone included Victor Young's theme to the Cecil B. DeMille epic *Samson and Delilah*, allowing her the chance to display her virtuosity as a classical pianist. Another classical piece opened *At Carnegie Hall*, a version of 'Black Swan' from Gian Carlo Menotti's opera *The Medium*. That Simone was drawn towards songs and instrumental pieces associated with films, shows and modern operas makes it even more difficult to categorize her, in that these areas of music do not represent styles so much as sites in which musical fusion had long been the norm. Perhaps this was one of the reasons Simone included a number of "show tunes" throughout her career, from early pieces such as 'Little Girl Blue' and 'Wild Is the Wind' to later examples such as 'Ain't Got No / I Got Life' (from the musical *Hair!*) and 'Papa Can You Hear Me?' (from *Yentl*). With 'Black Swan' and the two film themes occupying the first four tracks of *At Carnegie Hall* alongside Simone's own romantic love song 'If You Knew', it would seem as though the artist were going out of her way to prove she was not a jazz or blues performer. Other romantic songs followed – 'The Twelfth of Never' and 'Will I Find My Love Today' (both recent hits for Johnny Mathis) – and the listener has to wait until the medley of 'The Other Woman' and 'Cotton Eyed Joe' to come across the types of music discussed earlier in this chapter, jazz and folk respectively. An epic take on Nat Adderley and Oscar Brown's 'Work Song' (included on the "complete" edition of the *Carnegie Hall* album [B2] but originally issued separately) shows the band moving into what might be termed "soul jazz". Indeed, Simone's band – on this occasion, Al Shackman and Phil Orlando on guitars, Lisle Atkinson on bass and Montego Joe on drums and percussion – display a range of styles to match their leader's eclecticism. The guitar on 'Black Swan' is particularly revelatory; to contemporary ears, it is striking how the guitarist seems to anticipate a style that would become ubiquitous among the jazzier, exploratory end of Anglo-American rock and folk music in the late 1960s and early 1970s, for example the Grateful Dead, early Pink Floyd and Lee Underwood's work with Tim Buckley.

Listening to Simone switch from 'The Other Woman' to 'Cotton Eyed Joe' is to hear her as a radio dial, navigating the possible musics of her time. But it is more than this as the switch is carried so masterfully; Simone maintains a certain blankness in the vocal delivery of both songs that creates the flexibility necessary to match the seemingly disparate source materials. This is not the often cheesy showcasing medley that would become a ubiquitous feature of easy listening, lounge and cabaret singers. Rather, it is a highlighting of musical resonances that had begun with Simone's early fusing of pop and classical styles and would continue into her late performances when she would meld 'Mississippi Goddam' with Brecht and Weill's 'Moon Over Alabama' ('Alabama Song'). But if Simone is a radio dial, she is also a phonograph listener. Introducing her version of Lead Belly's 'Silver City Bound' (which opens Disc Two of the complete *Carnegie Hall* album), Simone says that she learned it from one of his records. It is a small but significant reconfiguration of the notion of tradition associated with the blues, at least in its more mythical form. As Simone introduces the song while sat at the piano on the stage of a prestigious metropolitan concert hall, having performed a range of film and show tunes, she seems a world away from the guitar-toting itinerant figures of Lead Belly and Blind Lemon Jefferson, the distance only exacerbated by her admission that she learned the tune in the domestic environment associated with the gramophone.

Conclusion

It is necessary to return to the idea that, as a multi-voiced performer, Simone ultimately defied category. But it is equally necessary to pause and think about what those categories are and how they are policed. For Simone, the answer to the latter question was that they were policed according to prevailing prejudices. A victim of various types of categorization, Simone was able to claim some measure of victory by her virtuosity and eclectic range. This eclecticism can be seen as political in the manner outlined by Nathaniel Mackey:

> [T]o the extent that categories and the way things are defined
> – the boundaries between things, people, areas of experi-
> ence, areas of endeavour – to the extent that those categories
> and definitions are rooted in social and political realities, any-
> thing one does that challenges them, that transgresses those
> boundaries and offers new definitions, is to some extent con-
> tributing to social change (quoted in Funkhouser 1995, 324).

The price Simone paid for this particular form of social change was to end up as a genre-less artist. Therefore, it remains an important task to recognize the contributions that she made to the established genres of jazz, blues, gospel and folk. By only classifying Simone as unclassifiable, we run the risk of over-looking these contributions.

One option available to us is to situate Simone in a wider context, one that saw the blurring of boundaries between artistic styles and high and low culture. This could be described as a postmodern moment, in which Simone participated as a postmodern artist. It was at least possible to consider what she did with 'Black Is the Color of My True Love's Hair' alongside what Burl Ives, Kitty White, Patty Waters, John Jacob Niles and Luciano Berio did with it. This moment in Simone's career combined a rush of success with exposure to an art world that could feed her intellectual and creative needs. Greenwich Village, at the time of her tenure there, was a utopian site that contained the promise for artistic, political and personal revolutions in the decade to come. As David Wild writes of late 1961, the time of John Coltrane's historic performances at the Village Vanguard,

> It's hard to grasp the amount of good jazz available to the
> Vanguard's audience in the Village that fall. The Five Spot
> had had Ornette Coleman's Quartet on-stage during the first
> weeks of October, and had followed it up with Cecil Taylor.
> Lennie Tristano and Lee Konitz were at the Half Note, and
> Sonny Rollins was at the Jazz Gallery – to name a few. For
> that matter, Ravi Shankar had offered a concert of Indian
> music only a month earlier (C10, liner notes).

At the time Wild describes, Nina Simone was fast becoming a regular feature of one of the area's other venues, the Village Gate, where she would record a live album the following year.[6] Considering Simone's connection with the Village, we may be able to discern a little better the ease with which the singer could follow her established strategy of performing music from a wide variety of categories. What I wish to highlight for now is Simone's involvement in a utopian moment – primarily based around Greenwich Village but extending beyond its borders – that served as both the seed of her future development and the hard kernel of her future disappointment. For, if this was not a decisive traumatic event in the manner of those described earlier – indeed, it seems as far from traumatic as it could be – it would become one later precisely through its exposure as unrealized potential. The potential offered by the Village art world and the potential offered by the civil rights movement Simone was beginning to become involved with at this time would be later conflated in the light of the failure of the latter to deliver obvious material changes to American society and of the former to lead to a cultural milieu where someone of Simone's uncompromising eclecticism might comfortably feel she belonged. In her autobiography, Simone would write, "Sometimes I think the whole of my life has been a search to find the one place I truly belong" (Simone and Cleary 2003, 113).

For now, though, there was still hope. This was the era of Simone's first "civil rights song", a reading of Oscar Brown Jr.'s 'Brown Baby'. Brown was one of the great black hopes of the time, a successful and talented young man whose 1960 album *Sin & Soul* (C6) had gathered critical acclaim and whose collaboration the same year with Max Roach and Abbey Lincoln on *We Insist! Freedom Now Suite* (C29) had launched a new musical challenge to the racial politics of the time. Simone had a place in both the aesthetic and political moment that such projects were in the process of shaping.

2 Politics

Introduction

In 1964 Nina Simone signed to the Philips label, for which she would record seven albums. The Philips period represents the middle section of the three major recording periods that made up Simone's prolific 1960s output, bookended by her work for Colpix and RCA. It is during this time that we find Simone's first major articulations of explicit political messages. If, as has already been suggested, Simone's defiance of category can be read as a political defiance, it is nonetheless difficult to measure the extent to which this was a conscious strategy that was undertaken at the time rather than a retroactive equation of musical categorization with social categorization and with stereotypes associated with race, class and gender. However, with the release, in 1964, of the album *In Concert* (her Philips debut), Simone stepped into the arena of political protest in an unequivocal manner.

At the same time, *In Concert* provided a sense of continuity with Simone's career to date. It was recorded at Carnegie Hall, as her final major Colpix albums had been, and it reprised three songs from her Bethlehem debut: 'Plain Gold Ring', 'Don't Smoke in Bed' and 'I Loves You, Porgy'. There was the usual eclectic mix of material, performed in the style that one *New York Times* writer had dubbed "Simone-ized" (Cohodas 2010, 104). What was different, however, was the inclusion of four songs that explicitly showcased Simone's growing commitment to the struggle for civil rights. These songs – 'Pirate Jenny', 'Go Limp', 'Old Jim Crow' and, most famously, 'Mississippi Goddam' – not only brought the civil rights struggles to the metropolitan concert stage, but did so in a way that foregrounded the incongruity of what was happening on the streets of the USA with the bourgeois milieu to which Simone and her music had come to be associated.

Revolution, Movement, Scene

In their book *Social Movements: A Cognitive Approach*, Ron Eyerman and Andrew Jamison use the term "cognitive praxis" to "emphasise the creative role of consciousness and cognition in all human action, individual and collective"

(1991, 3). It is this cognitive praxis, they argue, that transforms individuals into social movements and that gives social movements their particular meaning or consciousness, which might be understood as their relationship to knowledge (both worldview and particular micro-political agenda). At the same time as being constituted, social movements are themselves constitutive, bringing about major changes in how society understands itself:

> Social movements articulate new historical projects by reflecting on their own cognitive identity. In formulating their common assumptions, developing their programmatic presentations of themselves to the rest of society, in short by saying what they stand for, social movement activists develop new ideas that are fundamental to broader processes of human creativity (1991, 165).

They use the example of the American civil rights movement as one that created a new kind of self-knowledge in the country. The movement "recognized American society as fundamentally unjust, combining religious and legal consciousness into an integrated 'social gospel'" (165).

In his analysis of cultural trauma, Eyerman (2001) stresses the role of "movement intellectuals" in mediating between cultural and political spheres: "Intellectuals are mediators and translators between spheres of activity and differently situated social groups, including the situatedness in time and space. Intellectuals in this sense can be film directors and singers of songs, as well as college professors" (3–4). Eyerman and Jamison, recognizing their own indebtedness to the work of Raymond Williams and Antonio Gramsci, suggest that what is missing from many theories of social movements

> is a sociological concern with the actions of contextually bound agents, with what we have termed movement intellectuals and movement artists. It is here that biography meets history . . . [T]he life stories of key actors in the transformation of tradition – James Weldon Johnson, Langston Hughes, Zora Neale Hurston, Pete Seeger, Woody Guthrie, Bob Dylan, Phil Ochs, Janis Joplin, and Jimi Hendrix, to name a few – are central to our approach to sociological analysis (1998, 164).

I believe we should add Nina Simone's name to this list in that she exemplifies many of the ways in which "cultural trauma articulates a membership group as it identifies an event or an experience, a primal scene, that solidifies individual/collective identity" (Eyerman 2001, 15). This seems to me to be an excellent description of Simone's signature song 'Mississippi Goddam' and the *In Concert* album more generally.

'Mississippi Goddam' remains arguably Simone's most famous protest song and, not surprisingly, forms the basis for many responses to her work. Three powerful analyses of Simone's role in the politics of freedom of the 1960s (Feldstein 2005; Kernodle 2008; Brooks 2011) devote much of their space to discussion of the song. I wish to consider it by reflecting on the way that Nina Simone connected the song's composition to a subjectivizing event. In doing so, I hope to suggest, as in Chapter 1, some of the ways in which life, work, trauma and event come together in Simone's recorded legacy, a legacy that includes her autobiographical accounts in print and on screen as well as her sound recordings. The event in question dates from 1963 and is described in the singer's 1991 autobiography, from which I quote here at length:

> In Mount Vernon we had a little apartment built over the garage which was my private hideaway, where I went to practise and prepare for forthcoming performances. I was sitting there in my den on 15 September when news came over the radio that somebody had thrown dynamite into the 16th Street Baptist Church in Birmingham, Alabama while black children were attending a Bible study class. Four of them – Denise McNair, Cynthia Wesley, Carole Robertson and Addie Mae Collins – had been killed. Later that day, in the rioting which followed, Birmingham police shot another black kid and a white mob pulled a young black man off his bicycle and beat him to death, out in the street. It was more than I could take, and I sat struck dumb in my den like St Paul on the road to Damascus: all the truths that I had denied to myself for so long rose up and slapped my face. The bombing of the little girls in Alabama and the murder of Medgar Evers were like the final pieces of a jigsaw that made no sense until you had fitted the whole thing together. I suddenly realised what it was to be black in America in 1963, but it wasn't an intellectual connection of the type Lorraine [Hansberry]

> had been repeating to me over and over – it came as a rush
> of fury, hatred and determination. In church language, the
> Truth entered into me and I "came through" (Simone and
> Cleary 2003, 89).

Simone's first reaction is a desire for violent revenge for the atrocious events that have brought home to her the excess of her (and her fellow black Americans') situation. She attempts to build a gun in order to deliver retribution to the objects of her "hatred" and "fury". Her husband, a former police officer, discovers her and stops her, saying, "Nina, you don't know anything about killing. The only thing you've got is music." Simone accepts this and sits down at her piano:

> An hour later I came out of my apartment with the sheet
> music for 'Mississippi Goddam' in my hand. It was my first
> civil rights song, and it erupted out of me quicker than I could
> write it down. I knew then that I would dedicate myself to
> the struggle for black justice, freedom and equality under
> the law for as long as it took, until all our battles were won
> (Simone and Cleary 2003, 90).

As Simone goes on to note, when she started to become involved in the civil rights movement many already considered her an activist due to the publicity she gave to various aspects of the movement in her concerts and in interviews. She had already recorded songs such as Oscar Brown's 'Brown Baby' and her "Afrocentric" numbers from 'Zungo' onwards had asserted a "return to Africa" that reflected the emerging manifestos of black nationalist organizations. But clearly Simone felt it necessary, albeit in this retrospective account, to delimit a before and after, to hinge her commitment to civil rights upon a decisive event. Her positing of this event as both specific (the Birmingham bombing) and ongoing (the decision to commit herself to civil rights) reflects the process of "fidelity to the event" discussed in Chapter 1. That Badiou, from whom this notion of event was borrowed, should also have written extensively on St. Paul's conversion on the road to Damascus, only strengthens the relationship between religious and political conversion and commitment (Badiou 2003).

Indeed, conversion can also be read into the unfolding narrative of 'Mississippi Goddam' itself (B10, disc 1, track 7). The tune, in its *In Concert* incarnation (the first officially released version), starts off at something of a gallop, its uptempo rhythm seemingly eliciting pleasure from the Carnegie Hall audience, who laugh when Simone declares, "The name of this tune is 'Mississippi Goddam!'", pausing slightly before adding, "and I mean every word of it!" (to which the audience respond with more laughter). The opening lines – "Alabama's got me so upset / Tennessee made me lose my rest / And everybody knows about Mississippi / God-dam!" – are repeated, as if inviting a singalong, although it quickly becomes clear that this will be a difficult tune to learn as Simone changes the melody, slowing and stretching her vocals as she asks, "Can't you see it, can't you feel it / It's all in the air?" before circling back to the "Alabama / Tennessee / Mississippi" lines to conclude the song's first section. It is at this point that she issues the next interjection: "This is a show tune but the show hasn't been written for it yet", which is received with more laughter from the audience. At this point, we are just over one minute into this nearly five-minute performance.

There is a shift in the dynamics of 'Mississippi Goddam' here as Simone settles into the regular rhythm of what amounts, in this unusually structured song, to the first verse. The metre of the lyric stays constant for the next fifty seconds as Simone unfolds a series of increasingly stark images: "we all gonna get it in due time"; "I don't belong here, I don't belong there"; "me and my people just about due". The series culminates in the observation, "You keep on sayin' 'Go slow'". Simone pauses for breath as the tune maintains its momentum, then moves into a new section, calling out, "But that's just the problem", to which her band members respond with a shout of "too slow!". This response is issued after each of Simone's subsequent calls: "washin' the windows"; "pickin' the cotton"; "you're too damn lazy". As the song approaches the three-minute mark, Simone returns the melody to the "Mississippi God-dam!" refrain before offering her next spoken interjection: "I bet you thought I was kiddin', didn't you?" There is still laughter, though it is less audible and possibly more nervous than before.

The song moves back into the verse form for another series of vivid snapshots ("picket lines", "school boycotts", "all I want is equality / for my sister, my brother / my people and me"). Simone's vocal, earlier so playful and inclusive, has now become furious and declamatory. The lyric becomes ever more apocalyptic as she declares, "This whole country is full of lies / You all gonna die and die like flies", then uses the line "I don't trust you anymore" to return to the "too slow!" call-and-response section, which centres on key words of the civil rights movement ("desegregation", "mass participation", "unification"). As the song enters its final thirty seconds, it circles back to the opening tune, with Simone swapping the "Alabama / Birmingham" couplet for "You don't have to live next to me / Just give me my equality" and finishing with a drawn-out "Mississippi God-dam!", pounded home by pneumatic piano. As if the significance of the climax is not clear, Simone adds a punctuating "That's it!" and the band switch into Miles Davis's 'Milestones' to signal the end of the show.

In just under five minutes Simone manages to set a number of contemporaneous debates to music: an assertion of the "double consciousness" claimed by W. E. B. Du Bois as a conditioning factor of the black experience in America ("I don't belong here / I don't belong there"); a sense of desperation and an accompanying loss of faith ("I've even stopped believing in prayer", she declares at one point, as if the blasphemous "Goddam" had not already proven it); and the debates played out between various civil rights groups (CORE, SCLC, SNCC[1]) and black leaders (Martin Luther King, Malcolm X, Stokely Carmichael) over the place of nonviolence and armed struggle. Mirroring the shifting musical sands of the song, the position taken up by the narrator changes as she describes a growing sense that violence is the only option left and delivers violence upon her audience through the declamatory, performative nature of the lyrics (Brooks 2011). Simone cleverly combines what J. L. Austin (1975) described as "constative" language (that which describes facts or gives information) with "performative" language (that which does functional work: greetings, warnings, threats and curses).

What marked 'Mississippi Goddam' out from anything Simone had hitherto recorded were its anger, its sense of immediacy and insistence, and its strategies of alienation. As far as the latter goes, it could be seen as a successor to Billie Holiday's 'Strange Fruit', an invasion of brutal reportage into the polite environs of the supper club. The recording on *In Concert* would support such a reading, witnessing as it does a subtle but noticeable change that comes over the audience as the song narrative unfolds. But in other crucial ways, 'Mississippi Goddam' is a very different song from 'Strange Fruit' (discussed below), without the stillness and neutral, curious tone with which Holiday imbued her performance. Simone's is declamatory and insistent, closer perhaps to the cry placed in the title of the classic civil rights jazz recording, *We Insist! Freedom Now Suite* (1960 [C29]), on which the drummer Max Roach had collaborated with Oscar Brown Jr. and vocalist Abbey Lincoln.

As Dorian Lynskey (2010) points out, 'Mississippi Goddam' also echoes the voice overheard in the crowd witnessing King's "I have a dream" speech, a voice which responds to King's vision by crying "Goddam!" It is this declamatory quality that gave the song its power and that gave it a foothold in history, making it now seem both evocative of its time and continually, insistently relevant and disturbing. "Goddam" may have been a ruder, more shocking declaration in the Carnegie Hall atmosphere of 1964 than it would be today, but, because we know this, we can still witness the unsettling process of hearing Simone alienate her audience as the song unfolds. What is more, the decades that have elapsed since this landmark recording have done little to diminish the power of lines such as "you're all gonna die and die like flies".

As this line makes clear, 'Mississippi Goddam' is notable for its assertion of a desire for revenge, one that can be connected to the more vengeful parts of the Bible. If the statements were too violent to be categorized as gospel, the song nonetheless shares a predictive element often found in gospel. There is also an echo of the interplay between singer and audience that Simone used in her gospel songs, although "interplay" may be the wrong word, for what Simone often seems to do is highlight the barrier dividing herself and the audience even as she seems to invite participation. On the recording of 'Children Go Where I Send You' (discussed in Chapter 1) the singer alerts the audience to the recreation of a revival meeting while suggesting that they probably don't know what that is; so too, in 'Mississippi Goddam', where the breach is highlighted by the between-verse commentary ("this is a show tune but the show hasn't been written yet", "I bet you thought I was kiddin'").

Dynamics and Distanciation

There is a sense, in a number of songs Simone chose to perform, of working towards something apocalyptic. It can be heard in the threatening conclusion of 'Mississippi Goddam', in the bloody predictions of Brecht and Weill's 'Pirate Jenny', in the eschatology of Bob Dylan's 'Hollis Brown', in the declaration, in 'Sinnerman', of what will happen "on that day", in the gospel faith of 'New World Coming' and in the visionary polemic of Exuma's '22nd Century'. Whether via eschatology or the messianic, Simone managed to convey at numerous points through her career what James Baldwin, drawing on an old spiritual, referred to as "the fire next time" and Martin Luther King as "an idea whose time has come".

Such songs, loaded as they were with lyrical affect, offered Simone the chance to develop her sense of control over her audience. In this she also paralleled Martin Luther King. As Richard Lischer notes, King's style was characterized by the affective manipulation of pleasure in his political speeches and the use of "formulas" and "key-signature phrases by which he transformed the prosaic discouragement of his audiences into the poetry of a Movement". Lischer continues the musical analogy: "His audiences would cheer when he *began* one of his set pieces the way fans respond to the first bars of their favorite song at a rock concert. The formulas not only verified the identity of the speaker, they also guaranteed a collaborative role for the hearer in an important moment of history" (1995, 104, original emphasis). The role of the contemporary popular music performer has many connections to that of the political or religious orator (King, of course, was both), a point underlined in Simone's own description of the power she acquired when performing:

> It was at this time, in the mid-sixties, that I first began to feel the power and spirituality I could connect with when I played in front of an audience. I'd been performing for ten years, but it was only at this time that I felt a kind of state of grace come upon me on those occasions when everything fell into place. At such times I would give a concert that everyone who witnessed it would remember for years, and they would go home afterwards knowing that something very special had happened (Simone and Cleary 2003, 92).

Simone's performance of Bertolt Brecht and Kurt Weill's 'Pirate Jenny' provides a good example of the process she describes (B10, disc 1, track 3). The song appeared on the *In Concert* album and shared with 'Mississippi Goddam' a combination of situation and prediction. In both songs the gospel-like promise of future salvation was rendered as a violent uprising, or revenge, that followed a state of "going slow" and putting up with inequality. 'Pirate Jenny' originally appeared as part of Brecht and Weill's *Threepenny Opera*. Its narrative consists of the thoughts of the titular protagonist as she cleans and slaves for a group of "gentleman" in "this crummy southern town in this crummy old hotel". While the hotel guests ignore or overlook her, Jenny plots her revenge for the imminent day when "the black freighter with a skull on its masthead will be coming in". As the revenge drama unfolds, Simone veers between perky piano accompaniment and slow, drawn-out chords whose occasional dissonance echoes the dark thoughts taking root in Jenny's mind. Meanwhile, drama is added by the use of loud bass percussion whenever the freighter is mentioned, its effect being to give a sense of a dark storm brewing. The song is clearly a "show tune", as Simone had said about 'Mississippi Goddam' and she uses its changing dynamics to highlight the theatricality of the performance, moving between whispers, silence, screams and cries. This is most notable five minutes into the performance when, having established the arrival of the fateful ship and Jenny's new role as judge presiding over who should be executed, Simone cries "in that quiet of death, I'll say . . .", then stops, allowing silence to descend on the hall. Breaking the silence with a whispered "right now . . . right now", Simone continues to whisper the lyric, then to sing, as if in a dream state, in a soft voice with a hitherto unwitnessed purity of tone, about the departure of the ship with Pirate Jenny stowed aboard, the avenger's raspy grain only returning for the final notes: "on it is me".

This mastery of dynamic control – the audience sound spellbound – is what leads Russell Berman to conclude that Simone was aiming for aesthetic rather than political affect with her version of 'Pirate Jenny'. Her use of multiple voices and the relative ease with which the narrative of the song can be connected, in Simone's performance, to a "racial, regional, and class specificity", stand in stark contrast to the "crisp, mechanical", alienating delivery of Lotte Lenya, the singer for whom Brecht and Weill habitually wrote (Berman 2004, 177–9). However, Daphne Brooks (2011) takes issue with Berman's reading of Simone's Brecht performances, arguing that Simone achieved an affective distanciation both here and in the Brecht/Weill-influenced 'Mississippi Goddam' because her protest songs were so "other" and strange for the time in which she was performing them. By "distanciation", Brooks means a strategy of defamiliarization that aims at emotional estrangement rather than the mutuality of feeling expressed in many protest songs and civil rights anthems of the period. It is certainly the case that Simone created sides in her performances as much as she fostered inclusion. Brooks suggests that Simone achieves a "black female distanciation" that is notably distinct from other civil rights singers such as Odetta and Fannie Lou Hamer (2011, 179). The distanciation achieved by Simone was perhaps not that of pure Brechtian theory (which would also eschew the kind of emotionalism Simone was known for), but it did offer an alienation technique aimed at a society that had been conditioned to accept a range of stereotypical roles for black female singers (Brooks 2011; Griffin 2004).

Simone offers a different kind of distance in another civil-rights-themed song on *In Concert*. Her version of Alex Comfort's 'Go Limp' uses humour and pastiche to poke fun at the earnestness of much contemporaneous protest material (B10, disc 1, track 6). Comfort, a noted gerontologist, peace campaigner and, later, author of the bestseller *The Joy of Sex*, wrote the words to 'Go Limp' as a playful response to the CND marches in the United Kingdom. It was recorded by Matt McGinn for a version released by Folkways in 1963 and set to the music of a Victorian Music Hall number named 'Villikins and His Dinah' (the same tune, generally said to be Irish in origin, was used in the US for 'Sweet Betsy from Pike', as recorded by Burl Ives and others).[2] Comfort's and Simone's lyrics, describing a mother's advice to her daughter to protect herself from male advances while on a march, use a number of double entendres and anticipated rhymes to provide a humorous alternative to over-earnest accounts of marches and causes. The playfulness is supported musically by a simple, almost childish, progression that echoes the duplicitous naïvety of the song's protagonist, who deliberately misreads the nonviolent protestors' advice to "go limp" when being arrested as an opportunity to ignore her mother's advice in the face of a fellow marcher's advances.

Simone's version follows McGinn's, save for the substitution of NAACP for CND. She exaggerates the coquettish aspect of the song, reverting to a childlike voice both in the sung lyrics and in a spoken ad-lib when she forgets the words partway through; it is as if she is toying with the audience. In many ways, 'Go Limp' is a slight song when placed alongside most of the other material Simone was performing at the time. It is silly where her other songs are serious, pathetic or uplifting. It provides light relief in place of emotional resonance or deep thought. Yet it still takes part in the construction of a political space that is staked out along lines of distanciation, difference and surprise. As Ruth Feldstein highlights, the trilogy of 'Pirate Jenny', 'Go Limp' and 'Mississippi Goddam' positions a debate about nonviolence that resonates across *In Concert* (2005, 1362–5). As for distanciation, the fact that 'Go Limp' carries resonances of nasal country and folk music styles not generally associated with black female singers allows for a different kind of jolt to the expectations of Simone's audience (see Bowman in F5, liner notes).

'Strange Fruit': Billie's Bitter Crop

Billie Holiday began performing 'Strange Fruit', the anti-lynching song written by Abel Meeropol (under the pen-name "Lewis Allan"), in 1939 (C21, track 13). It was, as David Margolick notes, a difficult song to categorize at the time: "too artsy to be folk music, too explicitly political and polemical to be jazz" (2002, 22). Although jazz would come to be seen as a vital medium for the expression of discontent by the time Nina Simone came to record Meeropol's song, this was not the case in 1939. Dorian Lynskey identifies the newness and strangeness of 'Strange Fruit' in the way it alienated audiences rather than inviting complicity or solidarity as contemporaneous propaganda songs tended to do (2010, 5–6). Rather than aiming for collaboration, "the music, stealthy, half in shadow, incarnated the horror described in the lyric" (7). The artistry of the song (and of Holiday's timeless performance) has invited debates about the relationship between art, popular music and protest, something Simone would have understood very clearly in her self-written protest songs and in the artistic license she took with those of others. Years later, reflecting on her attitude to protest songs during the 1960s, she wrote:

> Nightclubs were dirty, making records was dirty, popular music was dirty and to mix all that with politics seemed senseless and demeaning. And until songs like 'Mississippi Goddam' just burst out of me I had musical problems as well: how can you take the memory of a man like Medgar Evers and reduce all that he was to three and a half minutes and a simple tune? That was the musical side of it I shied away from; I didn't like "protest music" because a lot of it was so simple and unimaginative it stripped the dignity away from the people it was trying to celebrate (Simone and Cleary 2003, 90).

Simone's attitude changed as she began to compose her own protest material and to politicize that of others. Like Holiday, she would take protest material into the supper clubs and, like Meeropol and Holiday, she would make it art.

Janell Hobson (2008), like Lynskey, notes Holiday's ability to avoid the potential pathos of 'Strange Fruit' and to avoid sentimentality through the use of ironic distance. Meeropol's words, for Hobson, fetishize the black body, which is "rendered metaphorically, even romantically, as 'strange fruit hanging from the poplar trees'". Holiday's vocal "bring[s] alive the poem's ironic edge by invoking the cynicism and despair that elevated the song from sentimentality to poignancy". This is achieved through moments such as Holiday's "sour" delivery of the word "bitter" and "the long, drawn-out off-key intonation of the word *crop*" (447, original emphasis). For her part, Simone moves between Holiday's ironic stillness and a more anguished cry (B10, disc 2, track 20). She offers a solo piano reading with little of the mercury virtuosity of many of her recitals, opting instead for slow-moving chords over which she stretches her voice, quiet at first, rising in volume at the mention of "black bodies swinging in the southern breeze", then dropping again. As the song progresses, she moves through sadness, poignancy and horror, the latter articulated via the shadow of her grainy breath, which is audible at certain points. At no point does she sound sentimental, although she manages this avoidance in a manner distinct from Holiday's. Where Holiday had adopted a distracted, flat and ironic ("sour") tone, one which meant that the potentially "voyeuristic" lines were granted an almost Brechtian alienation, Simone's is a more chiaroscuro reading, its light and dark textures unfolding the grim tale in the manner of a film noir. In the latter stages of the song, Simone starts to stretch the words to ever greater lengths, spending ten startling seconds on the word "leaves" (2:24–2:34). She saves the greatest amount of articulation for the final "crop", substituting Holiday's inquisitive articulation of the word for four swiftly traversed notes.

Simone's rendition of 'Strange Fruit', with its shift between flatness and depth of field, provides further evidence that, for her, blankness and the neutral tone were part of a wider set of performance dynamics that also included the sass of Bessie Smith and Ma Rainey and the controlled vulnerability (or vulnerable control) of Ella Fitzgerald, Sarah Vaughan and Maria Callas. Perhaps one of the reasons she insisted on identifying with Callas rather than Holiday was a recognition of the multiplicity of roles she could and would play, not only within a concert performance, but even within one song.

'Four Women': Between Worlds

As the foregoing has attempted to illustrate, Nina Simone's body of work is one in which issues of theatricality, history and identity, and a multiplicity of voices and roles, find representation. All of these are evocatively combined in another of Simone's self-written songs, 'Four Women' (B10, disc 3, track 13).

The song was first released on the album *Wild Is the Wind* (1965), although it clearly had a reputation prior to this album's release as it was deemed significant enough to be featured as the main title of the record, the font for the song being larger than that for the album title. Simone described the song as follows:

> The women in the song are black, but their skin tones range from light to dark and their ideas of beauty and their own importance are deeply influenced by that. All the song did was to tell what entered the minds of most black women in America when they thought about themselves: their complexions, their hair . . . and what other women thought of them. Black women didn't know what the hell they wanted because they were defined by things they didn't control, and until they had the confidence to define themselves they'd be stuck in the same mess forever – that was the point the song made (Simone and Cleary 2003, 117).

'Four Women' opens with a stately repeated piano figure accompanied by light percussion. Simone portrays the first woman by describing her black skin, long arms, woolly hair and strong back – "strong enough to take the pain / inflicted again and again". As she will do for all the women depicted in the song, Simone closes the verse by naming the subject: "What do they call me? / My name is Aunt Sara". Joined by Rudy Stevenson's gently insistent guitar, Simone repeats the name before going on to describe the second woman: yellow-skinned, long-haired Saffronia, the daughter of a black woman raped by a rich, white man. A few brief piano trills precede the description of Sweet Thing, a prostitute whose seductive charms are emphasized by a keening flute (played by Stevenson) behind Simone's vocal. The voice adopts a harsher, grainier tone for the final verse, which introduces a more assertive, militant figure, a brown-skinned woman whose "manner is tough" and who claims she will "kill the first mother I see". As all the instruments move together, Simone brings the song to a rousing climax, her voice rising to a shout: "What do they call me? / My name . . . is . . . Pea-ches!"

In addition to the evocative imagery that Simone uses in 'Four Women', much of the song's power comes from the symmetry of the four verses. Unlike the shifting metres and dynamics of 'Mississippi Goddam' and 'Pirate

Jenny', 'Four Women' builds its affect on consistency, each verse following what we might call the same "biometric" logic. To the same metric structure, the bodily features of each woman are outlined (skin, hair, back, hips), some historical or biographical detail is provided and, finally, a name is given. However, although the declarations that end each verse are delivered as first-person possessives ("My name is . . ."), the penultimate lines of each verse place emphasis on others' definitions rather than on self-definition: "What do they call me?" By posing the question this way, Simone's women are conforming to a representation under the gaze of others as described by Du Bois in his account of "double consciousness":

> It is a peculiar sensation, this double-consciousness, this sense of always looking at one's self through the eyes of others, of measuring one's soul by the tape of a world that looks on in amused contempt and pity. One ever feels his twoness – an American, a Negro; two warring souls, two thoughts, two unreconciled strivings; two warring ideals in one dark body, whose dogged strength alone keeps it from being torn asunder (1996, 5).

Double consciousness is most explicitly conveyed in 'Four Women' by Saffronia who claims to belong "between two worlds", but Du Bois's points are equally true of the other women in the song.

It is tempting to connect the concept of double consciousness to Nina Simone herself, given that types of in-betweenness seem to appear throughout her career. Not only was she an artist between, or beyond, categorization, but even her piano style evoked the sense that one was listening to "two different people – the bass player and the soloist" according to her long-time drummer Paul Robinson (E1). Her voice would also do quite different things to what her hands were doing, as, for example, on her rendition of Leonard Cohen's 'Suzanne', where the voice seems to be operating in a different time zone to her piano accompaniment (this double timing, wherein a slow or stretched vocal is overlaid on a fast instrumental or percussive base, could be seen as a derivation from African music). As if connecting her life experience to the way she played music, Simone placed herself metaphorically "between the keys of a piano . . . My secret self is between these worlds" (quoted in Cohodas 2010, 4). Simone's relationship with double consciousness is further complicated by her bipolar condition, which seems to have been the cause of much of the "capriciousness" (a self-description) witnessed in her interaction with audiences and industry figures, although to say this is in no way to deny the socio-historical factors to which Simone was subject. Rather, to note the coexistence of these splits is to emphasize again the interaction of the public and the personal, the collective and the individual, history and biography. Du Bois, like Frantz Fanon later, was keenly aware that the historical, collective experience of racism and colonization was something experienced within the individual psyche, while mental disorder always contains a social, public aspect, especially in a figure whose life is lived out in public. These relationships are also noted in the theories of cultural and historical trauma referenced in Chapter 1.

However, as tempting as it may be to read Nina Simone into one or more of the characters in 'Four Women' (Brun-Lambert [2009], for example, sees the women as representatives of different moments in Simone's life), we should also consider Simone as a "fifth" woman, exterior to the others. Seeing her as one (or all) of the women within the narrative reduces the longer historical dynamic of the song and neglects the importance of standing outside, of having a viewpoint that is not that of the victim. Peaches, for all her militancy, is still a victim and it is not her declamatory victory that represents Simone's power (though it can be certainly read as a representation of black power), but rather the distance that Simone maintains as a storyteller able to marshal *all* of these voices into a profoundly moving piece of sonic art. Arguably, we should not read any of the four women as representing Simone herself; instead, we should see them as finely wrought characters born of a great storyteller, one able to hold her audience spellbound while she narrates her tale. In addition to Simone as fifth woman, we might also consider other black female artists, storytellers and social movement intellectuals such as Lorraine Hansberry, Bernice Johnson Reagon or Angela Davis, the last of whom moved from a "Peaches"-like stance to a more conventional, academic role.

Furthermore, it is worth connecting other Simone songs to the concerns of 'Four Women'. One of these would be 'Backlash Blues', a setting of Langston Hughes's poem. The narrator of that song, who complains about a racist society sending her son to fight in Vietnam, represents another female role, the mother forced to watch injustice being visited upon her children (B18, track 14; Hughes 1995, 552). It sings of a world that is "full of other folks like me /

who are black, yellow, beige and brown", a reminder of the varying skin tones portrayed in 'Four Women'. The "backlash" of the song's lyric echoes the pain that has been inflicted upon Aunt Sara in 'Four Women', while also operating as an evocative metonym for the black experience in America and beyond. Furthermore, 'Backlash Blues' makes explicit the strategy that Hughes and Simone used to get their messages to as wide an audience as possible. Even in its basic form – that heard on the studio version released on *Nina Simone Sings the Blues* – it could be seen to package a subversive message into the familiar structure of the twelve-bar blues, as mentioned in Chapter 1. In live performance, however, Simone added extra commentary by introducing the song as a way of continuing Hughes's work and also including an extra lyric about Hughes telling her to "keep working 'til they open up the door" (B21, disc 1, track 20).

Another song that bears comparison with 'Four Women' is 'Images', Simone's musical setting of Waring Cuney's Harlem Renaissance-era poem of black self-identity. Simone would perform the song unaccompanied, as can be heard on the 1964 concert recording released on *Let It All Out* (1966 [B10, disc 3, track 10]) and seen on the *Live in '65 & '68* DVD (F5). To the silence and occasional throat-clearing of the audience, Simone chants the story of a black woman who is unable to realize her own beauty because the dull dishwater she works with (and, by implication, the rest of the world) offers her "no images" (Cuney's original title). The poet and singer can see the unnamed woman's beauty and imagine another life for her: "If she could dance naked under palm trees / and see her image in the river she would know". Unlike the dreamers and schemers of 'Pirate Jenny' and 'Mississippi Goddam', however, it does not appear that the woman of 'Images' has even had the dream, let alone begun to imagine it as reality.

If 'Images' sounded a note of defeatism, a subsequent Simone song asserted quite the opposite. 'To Be Young, Gifted and Black', co-written by Simone and Weldon Irvine, was performed as if from a parent's or elder's perspective, the kind of narrative that might have been passed on by one of Simone's 'Four Women' even if they were unable to realize its dream. Suggested by CORE members as the 'National Anthem of Black America', the song declares a need to alert black youth to their potential and their quest for parity. It was written with gospel music clearly in mind, with a choir employed to sing alternate lines with Simone's solo lead. A three-minute version following this structure was released by RCA as a single (B21, disc 2, track 13) and became one of Simone's most successful records. It was subsequently covered by Aretha Franklin and Donny Hathaway as a gospel-soul song and by numerous reggae artists, most famously Bob and Marcia, indicating the broad appeal of the song to artists from around the "Black Atlantic" (Gilroy 1993). In concert, Simone would extend the song to a much longer running time, as can be heard on the live album *Black Gold* (B7, disc 2, track 7). The singer introduces that performance with a tribute to her late friend Lorraine Hansberry, for whom the song had been written (the title came from a Broadway play about Hansberry's life). In this version of the song, the lines that Simone had sung solo on the single version are partly collectivized with the help of the choir though Simone's voice still stands out as she sings over or in syncopation with the choir). Simone takes a solo turn later, soulfully weaving in a lyric based upon 'Westwind', a song she had learned from Miriam Makeba: "make us free from exploitation and strife . . . west wind, with your splendour / take my people by the hand". She then settles into a repeated mantra – "unify us / don't divide us" – using the song as a prayer for freedom addressed to God and her mentors ("Lorraine, hear me . . . Langston, hear me . . . and help me"). The overwhelming impression is of Simone as a gospel preacher, both in command of her congregation and lost to the music and the moment, an impression made more real by the organ accompaniment. "Take this one home with you", she instructs the crowd as leader, band and choir return to the "young, gifted and black" refrain and the organ brings the service to a close.

Identity: Between Exceptionalism and Pluralism

In his meditation on the concept of identity, the Lebanese writer Amin Maalouf lists the many ways he could be seen to belong (nation, language, religion, culture and so on), before suggesting that "through each one of my affiliations, taken separately, I possess a certain kinship with a large number of my fellow human beings; but because of all these allegiances, taken together, I possess my own identity, completely different from any other" (Maalouf 2000, 19–20). This notion of a multiplicity that produces singularity provides a useful way of thinking about the often conflicting aspects of individual identity. It also points towards the politics of identity, in that it recognizes that there is a multitude of potentially conflicting affiliations jostling for recognition within any community. One way of contemplating the question of identity is to recognize that personal stories (autobiographies) cannot be fully understood without recourse to collective stories (histories) and vice versa. What is common to both is the quest for belonging, for working towards a sense of one's place and purpose in the world. Personal stories may dwell on issues of difference and heterogeneity, and histories on sameness and homogeneity, but this sense of place remains. Stories of communal identity have been written in various ways and around multiple shared properties but obvious examples relevant to this book would include those that coalesce around class, race and gender.

The songs discussed so far in this chapter have included those addressing specific publically shared, historical (often traumatic) events, such as the Birmingham bombing, and those of a more personal (which is not to say unshared) type, such as 'Images'. Songs such as 'Mississippi Goddam' were clearly aligned to anti-racist stances, while others, such as 'Pirate Jenny', while readable from a racial perspective, are connected to a broader concern with class politics. 'Four Women', 'Images' and 'To Be Young, Gifted and Black' are more obviously connected to "identity politics", a concept that would not have been identified as such at the time but which the 1960s were instrumental in bringing to public consciousness. This was an era in which, as has often been said, the personal came to be seen as political and what had generally been disparate political projects, such as the mobilization of the working class, the fight for female suffrage or the struggle for racial equality, came to be understood in ways more akin to Maalouf's description of multiple affiliations.

Maalouf's description of identity paints a fairly positive portrait of what we might call "identity factions". In reality, it has often been the case that different factions have been prioritized, neglected or pitched against each other in ideological battles. One such battle centres on whether race should be treated as an issue based primarily on biological factors and secondarily on social class or vice versa. While the types of categorization associated with race are supposedly biological, absurdities such as the "one-drop rule" that operated in the USA in the decades leading up to the civil rights era proved that race was as much a cultural construction as class. When Nina Simone protested, in 'Backlash Blues', against the "second class houses and second class schools" routinely forced upon the black population, she was tapping into a longstanding debate about the relationship between class and race that shows little sign of abating in the twenty-first century (Kelley 1996). Another debate which emerged from the black power and feminist movements of the

1960s was the marginalization of black women's voices in the representation of both race and gender (P. Collins 2009).

Common to all areas of identity politics are issues of essentialism and anti-essentialism. In brief, if one thinks of identity as being coherent, unified, natural and eternal, and one thinks of identity as being grounded in nationality, religion, class, race, ethnicity, gender, sexuality, ability, or any other quality, then one is likely to find some purchase in essentialism of one form or another. If, against this type of thinking, one wishes to emphasize lack of coherence, complexity, shifting identities and the play of differences, one is likely to favour anti-essentialist modes of thought. Much contemporary identity politics has favoured the latter approach, leading to an understanding where identity "has no clear positive meaning, but derives its distinction from what it is not, from what it excludes, from its position in a field of differences" (Robins 2005, 173).

As many have realized, the need to assert one's individuality may be diminished when one has alterity forced upon them or when one realizes that crucial identitarian battles remain to be fought: sides have to be chosen and stuck to, fidelity to one's people maintained. It is for this reason that many have found a need for strategic essentialism, the notion that, although one knows that nations, races or genders cannot and should not be reduced to basic essentials, there nonetheless remain vital reasons for imagining that they can and should in order to achieve a set of political goals.

It is necessary to highlight debates around identity in order to consider how Nina Simone was political on a number of levels. As we saw in Chapter 1, social categorization can be readily mapped onto musical categorization and vice versa. Even the simple act of deciding on and naming styles and genres is one in which strategic essentialism is frequently necessary merely in order for a music community to agree on what is available and where one might hear it. One of the challenges to socio-musical categorization is the argument that music, while obviously a cultural phenomenon, should not be explained solely by cultural means, at least not if those means emphasize negative social influences and neglect positive issues of aesthetic pleasure. Robin Kelley (1997), for example, has argued against accounts of black artists that attempt to conflate the traumas of racial politics with the creation of art. For Kelley, such approaches tap into a narrative that is always already suspect due to its assumption of an essentialized group:

> Conceiving of black urban culture in the singular opened the
> door for the invention of the "underclass". Once culture is
> seen as a static, measurable thing – behavior – that is either
> part of an old African or slave tradition or a product of dire
> circumstances, it is not hard to cast black people as patho-
> logical products of broken families, broken economies, and/
> or broken communities (1997, 9–10).

It is not that the "slave tradition" and "dire circumstances" have nothing to
do with contemporary black experience, but rather that care is needed when
making the connections. Kelley argues for a more complex, nuanced and
class-based approach, positioning himself against the white "neo-Enlighten-
ment Left's vision of emancipation which blames the emphasis on identity
politics for the demise of class-based analysis" (Kelley 1997: 12). Kelley points
out that an understanding of class always already necessitates an understanding of race, gender and sexuality. He is thus supportive of identity politics and
wishes to recuperate it from the critique to which it has been subjected by
those he sees as wanting to deny difference. Kelley's argument is a plea for
a consideration of African American art and culture along the axes of pleasure and aesthetics as much as those of social unease. He sees his work as a
defence of "victims of racist and sexist social science, social policy, and social
disinvestment" (ibid.). For him, too much social science posits black creative culture as a response to or coping mechanism of oppression and ignores
aspects of aesthetics, style and pleasure.

Soul as Strategic Essentialism

An example of the tangle of race and aesthetics can be found by considering
the word "soul" and the prevailing assumption that, whatever it might or
might not be, it is something that black people (though Kelley emphasizes
black men) are assumed to have. "At the very least", he writes, "*soul* was a
euphemism or a creative way of identifying what many believed was a black
aesthetic, or black style, and it was a synonym for black itself or a way to talk
about being black without reference to colour, which is why people of other
ethnic groups could have soul" (1997, 25–6, original emphasis). William Van
Deburg, meanwhile, devotes a whole section of his book *New Day in Babylon*
to a black-centred account of soul, soul style, soul music and soulful talk. For
Van Deburg it would appear that not everyone could possess soul:

As sung by the Beatles, 'Eleanor Rigby' and 'Day Tripper' were prime examples of clever mid-sixties Euro-American pop. The music was engaging, but contained not a hint of soulfulness. Versions of the same songs performed by Ray Charles and the Vontastics had it in abundance. The same could be said for Aretha Franklin's interpretations of hits by Simon and Garfunkel and Dusty Springfield. The singer, not the song, determined whether a tune would be considered soulful (1992, 207).

In such a formulation soul was, and is, something that cannot be defined but can be recognized when it is heard and, for Van Deburg, it can be heard differently in performances by black and white performers. The lack of definition is also apparent in Peter Guralnick's description of Aretha Franklin's version of the country song 'With Pen In Hand', which "sounds as direct, as enterprising, as freshly minted as her own compositions, the emotion welling up in a full-throated cry which, if not always supported by the weight of the words, uplifts, *in a way that cannot be pinpointed*, the mundane limitations of the text" (1986, 349, my emphasis). Rob Bowman (2003) analyses Franklin's version of 'Try a Little Tenderness' by contrasting it with the display of (white, male) mastery in Bing Crosby's version. Bowman attempts to escape the problem of merely claiming Franklin's version as soulful, submitting it instead to a scientific analysis. The contrast with Crosby, no matter how scientific, does, however, still pivot around the difference between Crosby's implicitly bland mastery and Franklin's explicitly "adventurous" embrace of "signifiers of emotional engagement" (2003, 116). Is *this* what soul is?

Connecting this issue to the challenge of categorization discussed in the previous chapter, it is interesting to ask to what extent Nina Simone should be thought of as a soul artist. Such consideration would seem to require us to focus on her 1960s music due to the ways in which soul was redefined during that decade. Although the word had been used by jazz artists in the 1950s and slightly later by crossover artists such as Oscar Brown Jr. (on his 1960 album *Sin & Soul*), "soul" came to have different resonances, both as a label for a style of music fusing gospel, blues and pop (and thus replacing the "rhythm and blues" tag of the previous decade) and as an assertion of political commitment (to the civil rights movement, to black independence and, in due course, to black power). Soul is relevant to the context of this chapter in both its attachment to black politics and its redefinition during the period under discussion here. It was during this period that Simone was given the title "High Priestess of Soul", a term used as the title of an album recorded for Philips (her last for the label). The album was recorded in 1966 but not released until the following year, which also saw the issue of *Silk & Soul*, Simone's second album for RCA.

Soul was used by some chroniclers of the black experience in the USA as a way of articulating a strategically essentialized notion of blackness associated with "soul power". However, while such strategies no doubt provided necessary affirmative messages during moments of crisis (and it can be convincingly argued that those moments are far from over), they also run the risk, when unquestioningly maintained, of ending in unhelpful self-typecasting. Can we claim that Simone was a soul artist just because she would fit many of the criteria established by essentialists (including strategic essentialists) who would equate the black nationalist/black pride rhetoric of which she was very much a part with an understanding of "soul power"? Can we claim her as a soul artist because, no doubt in an effort to capitalize on a contemporary buzzword, the record company that she was leaving (Philips) rushed out a record with the title *High Priestess of Soul*? Or because the record company she was moving to (RCA) followed up the album *Nina Simone Sings the Blues* with another entitled *Silk & Soul*? Or should we look to the music itself and claim that there is a certain soul style to songs such as 'I Wish I Knew How It Would Feel To Be Free'? Whatever the answers to these questions, Simone has remained a notable absence from virtually all popular and scholarly publications on soul music, just as she has from those on jazz, blues, gospel and folk.

Brian Ward (1998) suggests that "soul" was a kind of response to the political trauma of the times, a musical counterpart to the civil rights movement. While he is careful to note that music may not have actually changed things, he is keen to site black artists as articulators of a shared trauma. Who actually heard the message that was being articulated is another area open to debate, with Van Deburg for one seeking to polarize white and black reception of the music: "While blacks listened to the message in each song, whites were content to boogaloo blindly to the beat" (1992, 205).

There are crucial political reasons why such accounts as this, which sometimes seem to resist logic, are nevertheless important ones to pay attention to. It may be less important to attempt a taxonomy of soul – no doubt impossible, anyway – than to recognize the potential power that the designator "soul" can bring to music otherwise associated with dominant groups. As has often been noted, black musical innovations have often come about as a result of, and response to, an appropriation of prior black styles into the mainstream; what we might think of as a will to difference has driven black creativity and led to a situation in which what is done to musical form must both be provisionally named and moved on from. "Soul" is only one word to describe this process; "jazz" would be another, as discussed in Chapter 1. As Ben Sidran points out, "blues feeling" has also served this strategic role; following Lead Belly's definition of blues as a feeling, Sidran writes: "[A] ccepting the 'feeling' definition allows one to interpret the music as part of a larger cultural movement and to make distinctions between the use of the blues *form*, which many whites were employing, and the development of new techniques of blues *feeling*" (1995, 90, original emphasis).

Memory and Yearning

bell hooks (1990) addresses the sense of dislocation that has often accompanied identity politics via recourse to the concept of "yearning":

> Yearning is the word that best describes a common psychological state shared by many of us, cutting across boundaries of race, class, gender, and sexual practice. Specifically, in relation to the post-modernist deconstruction of "master" narratives, the yearning that wells in the hearts and minds of those whom such narratives have silenced is the longing for critical voice (27).

As an example of "those whom such narratives have silenced", hooks discusses the case of hip hop and the seeming conflict between the coming-to-voice of the black (generally male) subject and the postmodernist critique of the centred subject. It is interesting to apply hooks's articulation of yearning to the work of Nina Simone, not least as a way of recognizing the critical potential of the "sentimentalism" that Russell Berman saw as one of Simone's aesthetic triumphs. Yearning and longing, like the memory and imagination upon which they rely, are both tethered to place and able to place themselves as constitutive elements in memory as act and activism (Elliott 2010).

We can locate such an act of yearning in a suite of three songs performed by Nina Simone and her band at the Westbury Music Fair in New York on Sunday 7 April 1968, shortly after the murder of Martin Luther King. The songs were 'Sunday in Savannah', 'Why? (The King of Love Is Dead)' and 'Mississippi Goddam'. Simone begins the first song in what subsequently came to be known as "The Martin Luther King Suite" by expressing surprise that her audience have turned up to the concert hall given the tragic events of recent days.[3] "Happily surprised" that they have, however, she expresses hope that the evening's performance can act as some sort of healing ritual, or working-through of the mourning process. An elegiac note is struck with the languid 'Sunday in Savannah', a song which bears no direct reference to King or his murder but rather imagines a peaceful continuation of everyday life in a religious community, a practice, it implies, which King should have been able to pursue instead of having to take up the fight against an unnecessary evil. The longing here is not for what was but for what might have been had historical circumstances been different, had humankind been more tolerant, or had the dream that King foretold come to pass into reality. The sense of harmonious continuity is emphasized in the musical accompaniment by the organ (played by Simone's brother, Sam Waymon) and by the lightest of touches from piano, guitar and drums. Only at the song's culmination do voice and piano become discordant and harsh, as Simone substitutes "Atlanta" for "Savannah", invoking King's home town and pointing out "it's the same thing, same State, same feeling".

'Why? (The King of Love Is Dead)' was a song written by Simone's bassist Gene Taylor in response to King's assassination. As Simone says at the outset, the band had had just one day to learn it and the performance subsequently seems to veer between the rehearsed and the improvised. 'Why?' has made various appearances on record and CD, initially appearing in edited form on the RCA album 'Nuff Said (1968) and later being partially restored to its original version as part of the "Martin Luther King Suite" on the compilations *Saga of the Good Life and Hard Times* and *Sugar in My Bowl* (B19). The full, unedited version can be heard on the compilation *Forever Young, Gifted & Black* (2006 [B9]) and begins in a quietly elegiac tone as Simone introduces the song. Taylor's suitably epic opening – "Once upon this planet Earth" – sets the tone for a reverential account of King's life, work and dreams. To begin with, Simone stays clear of militancy as she emphasizes King's Christian message, the tragic sacrifice he was forced to pay and the possibility that he might have died in vain. Lateness is the song's keynote: King's lateness, Simone's growing sense of lateness (which would transform itself into a perpetual process of mourning, as I discuss later) and a general sense of lateness and loss for the civil rights movement. In one of the many unanswered questions of the song, Taylor and Simone ask "is it too late for us all?"

'Why?' can be heard as a motivated act of remembering, wondering and yearning. As remembrance the narrative is not inaccurate but, as with many elegies, accuracy is less important than the act of recalling a person's life and its meaning for a wider congregation. 'Why?' acts as a song of wonder and yearning simply through its positing of childishly simple, yet difficult-to-answer, questions. Why does it have to be this way? Why can't things be different? The black female voice, which Farah Jasmine Griffin describes as one of the "founding sounds" of the USA, has often been called upon to provide solace in moments of historical rupture. It is also a voice that "expresses a quality of longing: longing for home, for love, for connection with God, for heaven, for freedom . . . a conduit between what and where we are and what and where we want to be" (Griffin 2004, 119). Recalling Eyerman and Jamison's discussion of musical role models and spokespeople in social movements, it is clear that Simone needed to offer a response to the tragedy of April 4 and that those affected by the tragedy needed to hear from an artist of her stature, ability and socio-political position.

But 'Why?' does not consist solely of questions. To be sure, it manifests one of the commonly understood phases of mourning in its bewildered and uncomprehending whys, in its pain and numbness. But it also enacts another phase of mourning by showing anger and a refusal to accept what has happened. After seven minutes of Taylor's elegiac gospel song (closer, perhaps, to the kind of "sorrow songs" discussed by W. E. B. Du Bois in *The Souls of Black Folk*), Simone and the band start to raise the volume and the singer's voice takes on a harder edge as she poses a new question: what will happen in the cities now that "our people are rising"? Utilizing some of the stop-start drama of her reading of 'Pirate Jenny', Simone brings the searchlight of her voice to flash on "that moment that you know what life is", a moment of decision – an event – where the attainment of a new, more meaningful subjectivity is recognized, a commitment and fidelity that can survive even death. To a dramatically rolling piano accompaniment, Simone testifies that "you know what freedom is, for one moment of your life". As she returns to Taylor's lyric – "what's gonna happen / now that the King of Love is dead?"

– the song takes on a new, less fatalistic, more assertive dimension, no longer a question raised to a cruel God, but rather a threat and prediction of "the fire next time".

Perhaps not surprisingly, Simone also used 'Mississippi Goddam' in her Westbury concert to comment on King's murder and to connect it to other incidents, not least the church bombing that had inspired the writing of the song. At one point she replaces "Tennessee" with "Memphis", a reference to the city where King was shot; later, calling upon the audience to join her in song, Simone shouts "the time is too late now . . . the King is dead!" As if it were not clear that 'Mississippi Goddam' is delivering on the threats hinted at in 'Why?', Simone declares "I ain't about to be nonviolent honey!" Unlike the version of the song immortalized on *In Concert*, here it is Simone who is laughing. Her laughter seems as strange and out of place as that of the audience in the earlier version but we should probably hear it as an illogical response to an illogical and impossible situation.

'Who Am I?'

The questions posed by 'Why? (The King of Love Is Dead)' can be connected to those posed by a more general quest for identity, a quest which, it was suggested earlier, may be thought to begin with the question "who am I?" In attempting to answer such a question, one may have recourse to various discourses of the self, including those that rationalize existence through logical thought, those that look to immediate experience to situate the self, those that look to one's past experience (one's story, or autobiography), and doubtless many more. On recognition of oneself as a being amongst other beings, the question must inevitably become "Who are we?", from which one is led to those types of collective awareness subsumed under false consciousness, double consciousness and "imagined communities" (Anderson 1991), as well as the vast reservoirs of world history and social commentary.

It is to such collective accounts that the Nina Simone performances in this chapter most obviously belong, summoning as they do a critical politics of identity that engages with issues of nation, class, race, gender, sexuality and age. There are, of course, other modes of collective belonging to which Simone's art could be connected, one obvious example being religion and religious music. There are also an overwhelming number of songs of personal yearning, questing and belonging that make up Simone's repertoire, from the torch songs and blues of her early career to the sometimes nostalgic, sometimes bitter, songs of her later years. It is important to forge connections between collective and individual yearning, not least because Simone was a clear example of the personal as the political. As Michelle Russell notes, "[Simone's] most personal melodies (e.g., 'When I Was in My Prime' and 'Wild Is the Wind') always contained undertones of suppressed rebellion. When she began her crescendo, no one could ignore the dominant theme" (1982, 136).

In addition to explicit declarations of personal/collective identity such as 'Four Women', Simone provided some seemingly less serious answers to the question "who am I?" One of these is a version of Leonard Bernstein's 'Who Am I?' that appears on the album *Nina Simone and Piano!* The song's narrator, apparently more curious than her friends, who "only think of fun", finds herself wondering about predestination ("was it all planned in advance / or was I just born by chance?") and reincarnation ("will I ever live again / as a mountain lion / or a rooster or a hen / a robin, a wren or a fly?"). Lines such as "must I be the only one who thinks these mysterious thoughts" evoke the loneliness of the torch singer, albeit one with rather different preoccupations (past and future lives rather than lost loves), while the spiky solo piano accompaniment alternates between strangeness and pathos. On one level, the song can be heard as a kind of cosmic question that goes beyond any immediate situation (and beyond politics), as Simone was later to claim for her rendition of Sandy Denny's 'Who Knows Where the Time Goes?' (see Chapter 4). At the same time, however, it might be interpreted as an example of posthumanism, an example of what it might feel like to be free of the chains of humanity.

But perhaps this question ("who am I?") has not been formulated before the sense of recognition is forced upon a subject. There are numerous ways in which this process of recognition can be said to occur. In addition to those theories connected to consciousness (false, double, and so on), we might consider the psychoanalytic theory of Jacques Lacan, and specifically his account of the "mirror stage", in which one first recognizes oneself as an individual by imagining, via the mirror's unifying reflection, a sense of wholeness, distinctness and mastery which one does not, in actual fact, possess (Lacan 2006, 75–81). This misrecognition, for Lacan, is constitutive of subjectivity and we are subject to this fantasy of completeness for the duration of our lives, even as we attain greater control through our entry into the world of language, signs, communication and social interaction (what Lacan calls "the symbolic order"). But misrecognition may also come about due to a lack of opportunity to see one's reflection. In Simone's 'Images', the song's female subject is not able to realize her beauty because "dishwater gives back no image". This does not mean that there is no recognition, merely that the subject has had no chance to enter the fantasy of the mirror stage. She is still subject to the gaze of others, however, and to recognizing her subjectivity in the demands of others. She is, in this sense, a subject of interpellation, being hailed into existence through what Louis Althusser termed "ideological state apparatuses" (2008, 1–60), those cultural institutions that educate and inform us of our role in society and help to maintain society's power dynamics.

As much as the individual performances described in this chapter, Simone was able to set up a political space through the combination of material she performed. As we have already seen, 'Why? (The King of Love Is Dead)' was given a prominent position in a programme of songs dedicated to the memory of Martin Luther King. The power of accumulation can also be witnessed in a concert in Holland that was televised in 1965 (F5). The Dutch broadcast begins with Oscar Brown's 'Brown Baby' and closes with Simone's then-customary showstopper 'Mississippi Goddam', neatly encapsulating the political road she had travelled during the first half of the 1960s. Furthermore, all seven songs included in the set are representative of the art of politics that Simone was engaged in at this time. The songs are, in order of performance, 'Brown Baby', 'Four Women', 'The Ballad of Hollis Brown', 'Tomorrow Is My Turn / Images', 'Go Limp' and 'Mississippi Goddam'. Where 'Brown Baby' looks to the future and a time when it will be possible to walk down "freedom's road", 'Four Women' tells stories of the past and present, all narrated in the present because the stories have not ended and the ghosts that haunt the song are all contemporaneous with each other. Bob Dylan's 'Hollis Brown' narrates a tale of poverty so brutal it drives the starving Brown to end his family's suffering with "seven shotgun shells". Race is not mentioned in Dylan's lyric but, coming after 'Brown Baby' and the brown-skinned Peaches of 'Four Women', it is not difficult, in Simone's performance, to read racial inequality into the precarious existence of the Brown family. In her introduction to Charles Aznavour's 'Tomorrow Is My Turn', Simone says that she has turned it into a protest song. Certainly, the performance she offers here is more thought-provoking than the light, slightly too fast reading of the song that appeared the same year on *I Put a Spell on You*. Simone slows the pace and dwells on the forward-looking lyric in a manner that retains the optimism of the album version yet undergirds it with a sense of yearning and spirituality that adds layers of complexity and ambiguity. Performed in this manner and coming at the position it does in this set, 'Tomorrow Is My Turn' echoes the yearning optimism of 'Brown Baby', forging a connection that otherwise might not have been made. Rob Bowman hears in this performance of Aznavour's song "an unequivocal assertion of [Simone's] rights as both a woman and an African American" (F5, liner notes). 'Images', in turn, connects the nascent identity politics of the Harlem Renaissance to those of the civil rights era, Waring Cuney taking up his position alongside Oscar Brown Jr. in the vocal space created by Simone, a black woman who clearly knows and takes ownership of beauty. 'Go Limp' and 'Mississippi Goddam' add mockery and cursing to the set's political ingredients, the latter song serving as the ultimate meaning of its predecessors and as a barometer of the current situation.

Conclusion: Freedom Songs

The foregoing suggests that it is high time we add another category to those discussed in Chapter 1. That category is "freedom songs". In an interview for the film *La Légende*, Simone declared that, after her moment of conversion following the Birmingham bombing, making music that shouted out against injustice to her people "became the mainstay of my life – not classical piano, not classical music, not even popular music but civil rights movement music" (F1). This last term is in itself a good name for a category and would certainly encapsulate most of the performances discussed in this chapter. However, I intend to stick with "freedom songs" because it contains all the impetus of civil rights movement music while also referring to the generic and stylistic freedom Simone enjoyed through her musical diversity. It is, furthermore, a label that has been applied to her music by many critics and commentators. To speak here of freedom songs is to reassert the claim that Simone's musical diversity was itself as political an act as the explicit messages delivered by the songs she sang, and the performances and interviews she gave. In the words of Daphne Brooks, "Simone's social activism was not only incorporated into the content of her material, but . . . permeated the form of her musical heterogeneity that worked to free African Americans from cultural and representational stasis" (2011, 178).

3 Possession

Introduction

As we have seen, Nina Simone took ownership of her material via an assertion of identity politics, merging personal with political and individual pride with collective. This assertion manifested itself in songs such as 'Mississippi Goddam', 'Four Women', 'Backlash Blues' and 'To Be Young, Gifted and Black'. Ownership can also be understood in other ways when confronting Simone's work, for example by considering the importance of subjectivity and physicality in her songs. "Possession" is an appropriate word to apply at this stage, in that it maintains an emphasis on artistic ownership while also opening avenues of enquiry concerning the interweaving of agency and passivity in religious practice. As suggested earlier, Simone's strong links with religion encourage an identification of her concerts with church services as well as other ritual practices. The "church of Nina" extended beyond Simone's Methodist background to accommodate an interest in other religious activities from India, Africa and the Caribbean. Her interest in yoga or the spirits of Obeah might not have been connected to the specifics of their accompanying religions (in interviews she would often declare a belief in God but no adherence to a particular religion), yet it reflected a wider, and lifelong, spiritual search, itself a kind of possession. Simone's career can be seen as one in which issues of physical, mental and spiritual possession play out against or alongside one another in fascinating and mutually illuminating ways.

Embodiment: Malindy's Voice

One of the ways in which possession features in popular song texts is through the ubiquitous use of possessive pronouns, especially those in the first person: 'My Baby Just Cares For Me', 'My Man's Gone Now', 'My Father', 'My Sweet Lord', 'My Way', to select only from titles in Nina Simone's repertoire. While this is not the main aspect of possession I want to focus on, it does provide a useful starting point in that the use of first-person pronouns is one way in which singers and authors are connected to the narrators of song texts, the "I", "my" and "mine" of the song becoming conflated with those of the singer through a process of identification undertaken by performer and audience. Performers embody narratives and take possession of musical material. In a description of Nina Simone's 'Be My Husband' (B10, disc 2, track 13), Farah Jasmine Griffin focuses on the physical aspects of the performance in a manner which exemplifies this type of personal embodiment:

> At one point her voice shifts focus from melody to rhythm – keeping time like a hammer or hoe might have. Here she demands, there she pleads: She is both strength and vulnerability. When not singing we can hear an audible breathiness reminding us that the voice is situated in the body. At times she will substitute her voice with clapping hands, again embodying the song. Instead of hiding the breathing, denying the body of the singer in an effort to mimic an out-of-body spiritual transcendence, here we have a reminder of the relationship between body, breath, and spirit; a reminder that transcendence is acquired through the manipulation of bodily functions (chanting, singing, breathing, shouting, dancing) (Griffin 2004, 109).

Griffin is aware, however, that while such descriptions are apparently celebratory, they run the risk of over-determining the relationship between singers and bodies along gendered lines. Leslie Dunn and Nancy Jones (1994) argue that there is a long tradition in Western culture of locating the female voice within the body and connecting it to a natural state that is either pre-cultural or situated outside the male-dominated, masculinized cultural sphere. Griffin (2004) adapts Dunn and Jones's thesis to account for the historical representation of the black female voice in the USA, using as one of her examples the poem 'When Malindy Sings', published by the African American poet Paul Laurence Dunbar in 1895. The poem, written in black dialect, contrasts the unsuccessful attempts by a white woman ("Miss Lucy") to sing a song from a "music book" with the natural, untrained command expressed by the singing of the black kitchen maid ("Malindy"). Miss Lucy represents culture, education and privilege but all this is ineffectual when she attempts to create something beautiful and her efforts only result in "noise". Malindy, meanwhile, represents nature, humility and servitude but is able to attain a sort of freedom due to the sweetness and lightness of her song. The black voice, like the black female body, is essentialized in Dunbar's poem, nowhere more so than when the poet tells Miss Lucy "You ain't got de nachel o'gans / Fu' to make de soun come right" (quoted in Griffin 2004, 111), an observation that, as Griffin notes, connects to a long history of male narratives about the naturalness of the black female voice.

'When Malindy Sings' was set to music by Oscar Brown Jr. and recorded by Abbey Lincoln in 1961 on *Straight Ahead* (C27, track 2), her first album after participating in Max Roach's *We Insist! Freedom Now* project (C29). Brown's version does away with most of the dialect, not surprisingly given the change in attitudes towards the representation of black speech that had taken place in the arts since Dunbar's time. Listening to Lincoln sing Dunbar's words, we are offered the fantasy that we are hearing Malindy singing, that the representation of the female voice has been returned to the vehicle of the female voice. Even if, as was suggested with Simone's narration of 'Four Women' in Chapter 2, we do not imagine Lincoln as Malindy, but rather as a reporting voice, we can still note the transference of representation to a female narrator (Griffin's point). That transference may be only partial, however, as the division of labour is still weighted towards male representation: Dunbar's words, Brown's melody and Booker Little's searing trumpet solo, which threatens to steal the thunder from Lincoln's vocal and offer itself as Malindy's "voice".

Lincoln does at least bookend the song with two examples of wordless vocalizing that might represent Malindy's song. Nina Simone goes further in her version, recorded at the Newport Jazz Festival in 1963. As the lead instrumentalist, vocalist and predominant arranger in her groups, Simone would arguably always transfer the division of labour from its traditionally male bias even if she rarely performed with other female musicians. In her version of Dunbar and Brown's piece (B21, disc 1, track 8), we are more convincingly able to read Simone as Malindy because we also get to hear the song Malindy is singing. Simone's sense of ownership is established at the outset as she shouts out the key she wishes the band to play. She rolls out Brown's swinging chords on the piano to Al Shackman's subtle electric guitar accompaniment and offers a strident rendition of the lyrics that draws on Lincoln while asserting Simone's own voice, harsher and grainier. At 2:40, she starts to sing the line "Swing low sweet chariot" in counterpoint to the "Malindy" melody. While that famous spiritual had been referenced in Lincoln's version, it was only a line in the lyric; here, it takes on a form of its own, initially as a repeated intertextual reference, then, at 3:21, as an actual rendition of 'Swing Low, Sweet Chariot' with Simone moving into the chords of the spiritual. This lasts until 3:55, at which point Simone and the band move back into 'When Malindy Sings'. The switchover is startling in terms of the change in register of Simone's voice. As noted, her vocals prior to the medley section are grainy and harsh, but, as she sings 'Swing Low', she moves into a clearer, purer tone and lets her voice drift into more of a classical register, making melodic phrases out of particular words ("ho-o-ome" at 3:28 and 3:31, "chari-o-o-o-t" at 3:45). For a few seconds it is as if Simone has been possessed by the spirit of Marian Anderson, or what Michel Poizat might call a "pure voice diva" (1992, 180). Then, at the 3:55 switch, Simone proffers her croakiest, grainiest tone to sing the words "Malindy sings", an unmistakable shift of register that seemingly signals a move from character back to narrator. If the grainy voice *is* associated with narration and the clear, pure voice with Malindy, then neither Simone nor Lincoln are embodying her, but merely describing her. Following this revelation by Simone, Malindy escapes the essentialization of her "nachel o'gans" and is heard to be in possession of a highly trained, *un*natural voice. Following the deconstructive approach of Dunn and Jones's collection, this would seem to mark some sort of victory over the representation of the female embodied voice.

Physicality: Ain't Got No / I Got Life

As we saw in the discussion of 'Black Is the Color of My True Love's Hair' in Chapter 1 and of 'Four Women' and 'Images' in Chapter 2, the description of physical attributes forms an important part of some of Simone's most well-known songs. This physicality can be found throughout her repertoire, from the "hot hands" feared by the singer of 'I Loves You, Porgy' and the fingers counted by Little Girl Blue to the references to hair and skin in 'For A While' on *Nina's Back* (a 1985 album which also made physicality part of a bad pun with its cover depicting the artist sitting with her naked back to the camera).

Simone's most commercially successful celebration of physicality was her version of the song 'Ain't Got No / I Got Life' from the flower-power musical *Hair!* In a short version included on *'Nuff Said*, Simone spends one minute listing what she lacks – home, shoes, money, skirts, sweater, bed, mother, culture, friends, schooling, God – before spending the second, victorious minute listing what she has got: hair, head, brains, ear, nose, smile, back, sex, and more physical attributes, culminating in "my freedom" and "my life" (B18, track 18). A slightly longer version, included on *To Be Free*, adds brass and backing vocals to punctuate the lists and seal the message. The 1970 live album *Black Gold* features a version that lasts five and a half minutes, loosening the delivery of the first "ain't got no" half to dwell on its improvisatory possibilities, but returning to the tight groove of the second "I got" section to bring the performance to an apparent conclusion around the expected three-minute mark (B7, disc 2, track 3). However, the band resumes and Simone repeats the second part of the song, quickly at first, then slowing the tempo and reducing the song to piano, scatted vocals and ad-libbed lyrics, such as "I've got my soul, though it's been strained a little lately". Adding more lyrics concerning her commitment to her work, Simone leads back into the "I Got Life" groove to bring the performance to a close.

Physicality also plays a major part in the classic blues songs Simone performs, albeit via the use of metaphor and double entendre. Songs such as 'Chauffeur' and 'I Want a Little Sugar in My Bowl' liken the body to various objects, a practice also found in the more soul-based song 'Turn Me On', from *Silk & Soul*, in which the singer likens herself to "a flower waiting to bloom" and a light bulb waiting to be turned on (B15, track 17). 'Turn Me On' is also interesting in that it highlights the dynamics of desire and need, agency and passivity. While bawdy blues such as 'Sugar' or 'Chauffeur' mixed need with demand, maintaining a sense of agency for the singer, 'Turn Me On' projects passivity, the protagonist left in a limbo state as she waits to be brought back to life by a lover. "You're the one that turned me off," Simone admonishes at one point. "Now you're the only one that can turn me back on." Agency is not entirely absent – the musical setting (classic sixties soul) and the velvet voice ooze seduction, as if reminding the wayward lover of what they've been missing through their negligence.

This "power switch" trope is one common to love songs and religious practice. In the Methodist tradition into which Simone was born and raised, the role of preachers and music in "turning people on" should not be overlooked. James Baldwin powerfully combines these elements in his recollection of the Pentecostal church of his youth:

> There is no music like that music, no drama like the drama
> of the saints rejoicing, the sinners moaning, the tambourines
> racing, and all those voices coming together and crying holy
> unto the Lord ... I have never seen anything to equal the
> fire and excitement that sometimes, without warning, fill a

> church, causing the church, as Leadbelly and so many others
> have testified, to "rock". Nothing that has happened to me
> since equals the power and the glory that I sometimes felt
> when, in the middle of a sermon, I knew that I was somehow,
> by some miracle, really carrying, as they say, "the Word" –
> when the church and I were one (1971, 36).

Baldwin goes on to describe the process of epiphany as both a singular event in his life – his conversion to the church – and as an ongoing process in which the transportation from one state to another and the becoming-one of the congregation were repeated at each church meeting. We saw in Chapter 1 how Simone described this sense of power in her autobiography and, both there and in interviews, she often alluded to a sense of oneness on stage when, treating her audience much as she would a church congregation, she engaged in a process of musical transportation. An example of this can be found in two filmed performances of another song from *Silk & Soul*, 'I Wish I Knew How It Would Feel To Be Free'. The song, written by Simone's fellow North Carolinian Billy Taylor, works, in its basic form (which we might think of as the version on *Silk & Soul*) as one of many "freedom songs" written during the civil rights era that brought together aspects of folk, soul and gospel. The studio version provides instant swing with its rolling piano chords and finger-clicking intro.[1] Like the soul- and gospel-inspired compositions of Charles Mingus and Horace Silver, the instruments (here, Simone's piano and the simple click rhythm) seem to already be singing before any words are uttered, a feeling also present in Taylor's instrumental jazz trio recording (C37, track 1). However, it is the famously yearning words that connect Simone's version to the spirit of the times, becoming a collective anthem alongside Bob Dylan's 'Blowin' in the Wind', Sam Cooke's 'A Change Is Gonna Come' and the ubiquitous 'We Shall Overcome'. The key words and phrases in Dick Dallas's lyric – "break the chains", "remove all the bars that keep us apart", "every man should be free", "longing to live", "I'd soar to the sun", "I'd sing 'cos I'd know" – resonate with the classic freedom songs of the era. If the ever-present wish, with its seeming lack of fulfilment, sounds a melancholy note, the actual music sends a more affirmative message. Stabs of brass provide soul power and gospel clarification, suggesting that all the ambitions voiced in the song, the "longing to live", might just be within reach. It is even possible, due to the shift of the modal verb and Simone's articulation, to hear the repeated "I'd know how it feels" at the end of the song as "I know how it feels". Like many of the finest freedom songs, a certain amount of ambiguity refuses a closed meaning and allows for the imagination of utopian space.

At the same time, for all the song's collective message, it is always possible to read other messages into Simone's performances and to see certain songs as vehicles for connecting different aspects of the artist's life. In a filmed performance of 'I Wish I Knew' used in Joel Gold's film *Nina* (F2), Simone slows the tempo and opens the song space by adding improvised elements. As the crowd clap and shout affirmative messages in response to Simone's clearly articulated vocals, the concert takes on the atmosphere of a religious revival meeting. At the point where the artist embarks on a jazz-influenced piano solo, Gold's editor Frederick Charney intercuts material from a filmed interview in which Simone describes such meetings: "Nothing stops happening until everyone in the room is satisfied . . . there's no such thing as the end [of a song]." In a manner similar to Baldwin, Simone describes the interactive nature of song performance in revivals as "like being in touch with a hundred or 200 human beings at one time . . . that's a fantastic thing". Cutting back to the concert performance, we witness Simone improvising additional wishes to Dallas's lyric ("I'd sing so much better . . . I'd dance so much better . . . I'd be a little less mean") as a call to the band's response. To enthusiastic audience feedback, she testifies to a dream of flying and speaks of having her eyes opened to a "new vision". Having now assumed the role of gospel preacher, Simone continues: "The Bible says 'be transformed by the renewing of your mind'", then jumps up from her piano stool to take a position at the front of the stage, swaying with the music, screaming, clapping and leading her congregation. Returning to the piano, she sings about a moment in her life when she would know the feeling of freedom, stretching the final "free!" over several seconds. The phrase "for one moment in my life" resonates with her use of almost identical words during the contemporaneous "Martin Luther King Suite" ("for one moment of your life"), connecting to that testimony and showing how Simone, like King, used particular "formulas" and "key-signature phrases" as part of her affective work (Lischer 1995, 104).

In an earlier section of Gold's film, Simone attempts to answer a question posed by an interviewer: "What is 'free' to you?" In response, she describes a feeling she occasionally gets on stage, then clarifies freedom as "no fear" and "something to really really feel . . . like a new way of seeing". With the help of Gold and Charney, Simone is able to take possession of Taylor and

Dallas's song, connecting it to her religious background and to the freedom she sought in performing music. At the same time, the freedom she describes involves giving herself over to a situation that is larger than she or any one individual, one that is created through religious possession and group psychology. The "new way of seeing" echoes other statements Simone made about St. Paul-like moments of "coming through" or "turning on", suggesting she attained (and was taken over by) a new subjectivity in response to such epiphanies. For Badiou, who sees in St. Paul an example of a subjectivity based upon recognition of universal truth, the realization engendered by epiphany is one which, through the processes of fidelity, searching and constant renewal, allows the subject to reject conformity. Badiou uses the same words of Paul quoted by Simone – "Do not be conformed to the present century, but be transformed by the renewal of your thought [mind]" (Romans 12:2) – to highlight the universalism that, for Badiou, is Paul's greatest legacy:

> Far from fleeing from the century, one must live with it, but without letting oneself be shaped, conformed. It is the subject, rather than the century, who, under the injunction of his faith, must be transformed. And the key to this transformation, this "renewal", lies in thought (2003, 110).

Freedom, then, can be gained through nonconformity, and thought – the quest for the knowledge of how it would feel – is the first step towards freedom.

Another filmed performance of 'I Wish I Knew How It Would Feel To Be Free' combines the religious aspects mentioned above with a kind of embodying of the song that, paradoxically, allows the singer to break free of her own body for a fleeting moment and to suggest that one of the freedoms promised is, in fact, freedom from bodily determinism. The performance comes from Simone's 1976 appearance at the Montreux Jazz Festival, a concert discussed in more detail later in this book. Simone begins the song with the familiar piano motif, not deviating far from the recorded version, although she extends the pre-vocal section as if to get into the groove (F3). The subsequent rendition also follows the recorded version, save for a few interjections, a greater amount of jazz phrasing on the vocals and some harsh piano stabs (something of a Simone trademark, deployed at strategic punctuating moments and very frequently at the close of songs). The changes come towards the end of the song, the first being when Simone shifts into falsetto as she imagines being a bird, her voice soaring with the lyric to a height all the more notable for her infrequent use of such high pitch. For a few moments it is as if she really is breaking free of anything in the song that might be binding her, even the very thing that makes singing and playing possible, the music itself. "Spirit's movin' now", Simone observes, realizing the new freedom she has found and connecting it to a religious notion of transcendence. As if confirming the confusion over whether she originally sang "I'd know how it feels" or "I know how it feels", she testifies to the latter as she improvises new lyrics and interjections: "Got news for you. I already know . . . Jonathan Livingston Seagull ain't got nothing on me". She shouts the word "free!" four times in succession, then develops it into "I'm free and I know it". Changing to a new, seemingly improvised tune, Simone sing-speaks the truth she's discovered: "I found out how it feels not to be chained to any thing, to any race, to any faith, to anybody, to any creed, to any hopes, to any anything". Again, we could read this "religiously", seeing this freedom as an escape from earthly concerns, even from the body itself. However, given the denial of faith and creed here, it is equally tempting to connect the perform-ance to the identity politics discussed in the previous chapter and further-more to the kind of performance of identity that Judith Butler would later write about (Butler 1999).

I Put a Spell on You: Possessing/Being Possessed

In addition to her influential work on the performance of identity, Butler has also written on mourning in ways that are useful for setting up another under-standing of "possession". To a certain extent, the discussion of religion above has already begun to explore this understanding in that we have seen that per-formance can involve both taking possession *of* something – explored above as embodiment and below as authorial ownership – and being possessed *by* something. This dual aspect of possession, common to studies of religious and ritual practices, can also be seen in other aspects of everyday life. It is there, for example, in the everyday practice of consumption, in the way that the acquisition and consumption of possessions can turn us into consumed beings, at the mercy of all manner of temptations and unquenched desires. It is there, too, in moments of insight gained through experience of gain and loss, through epiphanies (which do not need to be religious in origin, though we may use religious language in describing them) and the challenges faced by showing fidelity to the truths illuminated by epiphanies. Writing on loss, Butler states: "Something takes hold of you: where does it come from? What sense does it make? What claims us at such moments, such that we are not the masters of ourselves? To what are we tied? And by what are we seized?" (2004, 21). The servitude Butler is describing is the realization that the truth glimpsed in the epiphanic moment may never be repeated. The mourning engendered by such realization is one in which the subject agrees to be possessed by loss, to willingly give up agency: "Perhaps . . . one mourns when one accepts that by the loss one undergoes one will be changed, possibly for ever. Perhaps mourning has to do with agreeing to undergo a transformation (perhaps one should say *submitting* to a transformation) the result of which one cannot know in advance" (21, original emphasis).

Such language – submission, transformation, possession – is not far removed from that of the religious performances already discussed; Butler's description of transformation echoes Baldwin's. It is also redolent of other types of religious practice found across the world and to the performance of music. Indeed, it was by combining such elements that Nina Simone earned the nickname "High Priestess of Soul", even if it was a label she distanced herself from. It is worth briefly considering "weak" connections with religious practices other than those of Simone's Baptist and revivalist background to shed some light on the dual nature of possession as manifested in musical performance. Those practices are Voodoo and Obeah and the connections are described as "weak" merely because I do not believe that the performers mentioned here – Screaming Jay Hawkins, Exuma and Nina Simone – could be taken seriously as representatives, let alone practitioners, of voodoo or Obeah. Rather, they have taken elements from these practices in order to fashion them into popular entertainment. The connections are, I believe, still worth making for the light which may be shed on the dual nature of possession and on the use of declamatory styles, damning and cursing in popular song texts.

Screaming Jay Hawkins's 'I Put a Spell on You', in its original form, would have been a fairly straightforward rhythm and blues number had it not been for Hawkins's bizarre vocal interjections and grunts, his ghostly laugh, his performance style and general "voodoo machismo" (Middleton 2006, 120). It was these factors – the capes, the bones in the nostrils, the coffins and the "skull stick" – that came to be associated with what one recent compilation termed "voodoo blues" (D6). Hawkins's song made no mention of voodoo, or the distantly related hoodoo that had been a feature of blues recordings dating back to Ma Rainey's 'Louisiana Hoo Doo Blues', but its evocative use of the word "spell" helped to forge a connection. Emerging in the 1950s, the song took its place amongst the more general world of "exotica" exemplified by Martin Denny, Les Baxter and Arthur Lyman.

Simone's version of 'I Put a Spell on You' does not summon up a voodoo ceremony, nor engage in exotic imaginings. It opens instead with lush strings reminiscent of one of the singer's show or film tunes (B10, disc 2, track 1). However, the voice, when it enters, is harsh, rasping, shouting, scatting and demanding: "You better stop the things you do". As Simone repeats the line "I ain't lyin'", a harp plays behind her and the strings swell. A struggle develops between the gentle backing and the harsh voice. As if intervening in the debate, a saxophone stutters a solo, driving the singer to a further sense of distress as she scats her way into a repeated "I love you" before offering herself as a possession: "I don't care if you don't want me / I'm yours right now". But this offering of herself is staged in a manner that drips with agency, control and command: "do you hear me? I put a spell on you . . . because you're mine". This combination of active and passive, subject and subjected, is given its most powerful reading in this closing line, which, as vocalized by Simone, veers from Hawkins's lyric into an untranscribable agglomeration of sounds that are less scat singing than a kind of vocal possession, a speaking in tongues. Ultimately, despite the stately music to which Simone's version of the song is set, the vocal maintains as much ritual power and strangeness as the original.[2]

Simone would work with similar magic on the Obeah-influenced songs she borrowed from Exuma. Born Tony McKay, Exuma was a Bahamian artist who had been active in the Greenwich Village scene in the 1960s and who later released a series of albums in which he presented himself as a singer-priest known as the "Obeah man". It is not clear where Simone encountered Exuma's work but she recorded three of his songs, 'Dambala', 'Obeah Man' and '22nd Century'. Simone reworked 'Obeah Man' as 'Obeah Woman', effectively taking on Exuma's role as priest(ess). The live performance that appears on *It Is Finished* (recorded in 1973 and released the following year) opens with polyrhythmic percussion from Babatunde Olatunji and Simone asserting that she wishes to take her time "gettin' this one together" (B7, disc 1, track 11). As the groove establishes itself, Simone tells her audience that she has "gotta go home", asking them, "Do you know 'bout the Holy Roller

Church? Ain't that where I started?" To enthusiastic audience response, she claims "I've outgrown it now . . . I'm so proud that I did it . . . that I came through." The references are ones she would later elaborate on in her autobiography. Although her mother had been a Methodist minister, Simone had favoured the music of the Holiness church (the "Holy Rollers") because "their prayer meetings were one great commotion, with people testifying and shouting all night. The music that went along with it had incredible rhythm, it sounded like it came straight out of Africa" (Simone and Cleary 2003, 17).

"Home", then, would seem to possess at least a double meaning for Simone when she came to perform 'Obeah Woman', referring to both her childhood home of Tryon and the imagined and longed-for home of Africa (not long after this performance was recorded, Simone would move to Liberia). As she eases into the song, she seems keen to educate her audience: "do you know what an Obeah woman is?" To affirmative response she launches her version of Exuma's lines: "I'm the Obeah woman, from beneath the sea / To get to Satan, you gotta pass through me". The crowd roar their approval and clap along to the hypnotic beat. Simone continues, interweaving Exuma's mythic lines with asides that clearly refer to her own life experience: "they call me Nina, and Pisces too / There ain't nothin' that I can't do", the latter appended with the ambiguous agency of "If I choose to . . . If you let me". Indeed, 'Obeah Woman' plays out as a classic example of the double nature of possession already alluded to; in order to offer the illusion of power, control and affective dominance, Simone needs to give herself over to the driving, possessive force of the "percussive field" (Mowitt 2002) and, even more, to the audience's approval (signalled by shouted responses, handclaps and, presumably, body language), effectively making herself a vehicle through which the spirit of the performance, its Obeah, can be channelled. "I didn't put that name on myself", Simone confides after six minutes of possessed performance, "and I don't like it sometimes". As if realizing the façade could easily crumble, she suddenly commands her musicians to finish. The abruptness of the ending serves as indication of the fragility and liminality of the songspace. Just as the Obeah woman is a gatekeeper between the world above and that below, so she guards the sacred space opened up by the groove of 'Obeah Woman'. When the song is "open" it can act as a conduit for a crossing over, coming through or loss of self; when closed it remains only as memory of an epiphany.

Although the spectre of the slave haunts many of Simone's narratives, it is arguably given its greatest articulation on 'Dambala', another Exuma song performed by Simone during the same concert in which she performed 'Obeah Woman' (B7, disc 1, track 9). This avenger's song consists of an invocation of Dambala and a set of curses aimed at those who would take ownership of others: "You slavers will know what it's like to be a slave". The main accompaniment is a sitar, which stands out given its rarity on Nina Simone recordings. Simone uses her piano and voice to add harshness and intensity as she strengthens the curses: "You'll remain in your graves with the stench and the smell". She drops to her softest tone to call on Dambala again, then closes the song with a heartstopping silence. The hypnotic tone, combined with the quiet/loud dynamics, limbo-referencing lyric and unusual instrumentation, lend the song an otherworldly feel; Mike Butler writes of the performance that it "visits a place beyond death" (B7, liner notes). It is an effective description, though I would argue that, as with many of the performances described here, it visits that place between life and death staked out by possession.

Agency: The Other Woman

We have seen how Simone's performances of 'I Put a Spell on You' and 'Obeah Woman' communicate messages of agency and passivity, ownership and submission. A related dynamic can be found in 'The Other Woman', a song Simone performed throughout her career and which brings together aspects of physicality with the deceptive passivity of the torch song (B10, disc 3, track 2). In fact, the song is only superficially torch-like. The first verses compare the physical attributes of "the other woman", the narrator's rival who "finds time to manicure her nails", who "is perfect where her rival fails" and who, it initially appears, is the one favoured by the man in the song. A triangle is set up of a desirable, cheating husband, a faithful but unglamorous wife and mother painfully aware of her husband's infidelity, and the "perfect" lover. This scenario of an abandoned woman comparing herself to a rival and staying faithful to her man despite his betrayal would not be out of place in a torch song. The sadness of Simone's tone and the pathetic piano accompaniment appear to underline an interpretation of the song as one of passivity and submission. However, there are clues, even before the song enters its second phase, that the glamorous lover, described at one point as a "lonesome queen", does not necessarily hold the upper hand; we are told, for example, that her time with the husband is "a change from old routine".

This aspect then becomes the focus of the song as it hinges on the crucial word "but" (which Simone stretches to several beat-less seconds on most recorded performances). "Bu-uh-uh-uh-uh-uh-uh-uh-ut", we are told, "the other woman / will always cry herself to sleep" and "will never have his love to keep". Her ultimate destiny is to spend her life "alone", a word given extra emphasis on *Let It All Out* being preceded by one of Simone's (at that time) trademark scats and underlined by a variation of the "Wenceslas" theme that Simone regularly wove into 'Little Girl Blue'. The relish given to this finale suggests a kind of revenge enacted by the song's narrator. She may not be the victor (if anyone is, it is surely the husband, who escapes the song unscathed and still desired), but the element of justice and/or revenge connects the song to a tradition that has more in common with the sometimes ambiguous feminism of country music than with the submissive stance of the torch song. Common to both traditions, however, is a sense of transition from suffering, subjected lover to singing subject in control of the situation and its narrativization. If history is written by the victors, the narrative signals some sort of victory over fate, the singing of it even more so.

Covers

We have already seen how Simone connects to another type of possession by interpreting and refashioning pre-existing material. As Richard Middleton notes, the application of Simone's qualitatively "constant" voice to others' material "can be regarded as already a kind of authorial gesture, pulling the material into her own orbit where it pretty much circles round this voice" (2006, 118; see also Friedwald 2010, 414). Perhaps Simone's identification with Maria Callas rather than Billie Holiday resulted partly from a desire to be seen as a vocal actor rather than a communicator of personal angst. This would seem to fit with her adoption and adaptation of numerous song genres. While Simone's early career saw her tackling material from the mid-century songbooks of classic songwriters rather than performers, she increasingly turned her attention to the newly emerging songbooks of the post-Beatles era, singer-songwriters such as Bob Dylan, Leonard Cohen, and the Gibb brothers (known in their performing capacity as the Bee Gees), Jimmy Webb and Randy Newman.

To begin to ascertain and understand the qualities of Simone's late voice, as I intend to do in the next chapter, it will be useful to first measure the extent to which her appropriations of contemporary material can be seen as victorious ones. Below, I discuss a selection of Bob Dylan tracks, some of which will allow us to connect this aspect of possession (appropriation of others' material) with an earlier one (embodiment). After discussing the Dylan songs, I examine Simone's readings of Leonard Cohen's 'Suzanne' and Paul Anka's 'My Way'.

Simone's Dylan

The impression that Simone was a prolific interpreter of Bob Dylan's work comes mainly from the fact that three of his songs were included on the 1969 album *To Love Somebody*. Outside of this concentrated dose of Dylan, Simone's official discography contains just two songs written by him ('The Ballad of Hollis Brown' on 1966's *Let It All Out* and 'Just Like a Woman' on 1971's *Here Comes the Sun*). We cannot, then, imagine a concept album along the lines of *Sings Billie Holiday* or *Sings Ellington*, but the five selections still provide an interesting perspective on Simone as interpreter. Here I will focus on the three songs to be found on *To Love Somebody* and which accounted for three quarters of that album's B-side (the other song being a version of the Bee Gees' 'I Can't See Nobody'). This Dylan suite began with 'I Shall Be Released', one of Dylan's most gospel-like compositions and one which, to a certain extent, remains known more through cover versions than through Dylan's own. Dylan recorded the song with The Band in 1967 for what became known as the "basement tapes", named after the basement of the house in Wood-stock, New York where the sessions took place. The song signalled something of a departure for Dylan following the turmoil of the recent "electric" period during which he had reinvented himself as a rock star, rewritten the rules of rock songwriting and angered many of his erstwhile folk audience by aban-doning the concerns of the civil rights era. The songs written and recorded by Dylan and The Band during their rural retreat from the media glare harked back to the older styles of music they had initially been inspired by, a mix-ture of folk, blues, jazz, country, medicine show songs and early rhythm and blues. Gospel music was another influence that shone through, no more so than on 'I Shall Be Released', with its visionary, yearning references to shin-ing light and escape from bondage. While the lyric remained secular – the hopes and dreams of a wrongly convicted prisoner – the metaphors of light and freedom resonated with those of other freedom songs, and the fal-setto vocals of The Band's Richard Manuel, sailing in over Dylan's (at that time) surprisingly gentle, aching tones, encouraged a more spiritual reading.

When The Band came to record their first official album *Music from Big Pink* in 1968, the distinctive way in which they layered their voices was, according to guitarist Robbie Robertson, influenced by gospel groups such as the Staple Singers (C2, liner notes).[3] The album included another version of 'I Shall Be Released', this time featuring Manuel's yearning falsetto foregrounded in the mix, which, in combination with the liberty-focused lyric, conveyed the kind of gospel-influenced singing made famous by Sam Cooke. The otherworldly feeling is enhanced by the use of a distorted electric keyboard, which gives a spacey rising and falling sound, a psychedelic spiritual.

Given the gospel associations of 'I Shall Be Released', it is perhaps not surprising to hear the song included on an album of Dylan covers by gospel group The Brothers & Sisters in 1971 (C5). On *Dylan's Gospel*, the song is given a full-blown gospel treatment, with the choir repeating back lines of the verses and taking over the vocal for key phrases (such as "I see my light come shining") and at the chorus, while a churchlike atmosphere is maintained through the use of an organ to complement the piano. Given that the group (which was seemingly put together for this project) give comparable readings to nine other Dylan compositions – including the secular 'Lay Lady Lay', 'I'll Be Your Baby Tonight' and 'Just Like a Woman' – we should perhaps not see 'I Shall Be Released' as singular in its potential for gospelization, though it is probably one of the most convincing performances on the album due to its inherently sanctified feel.

Nina Simone's version of the song (B22, track 6) begins somewhat surprisingly with Al Shackman laying a blues progression over Simone's piano runs, conjuring a sound not unlike that used on *Nina Simone Sings the Blues*. This impression is dispelled as the band move into a performance that falls somewhere between that of The Band and of The Brothers & Sisters. As Simone intones the first verse, female backing vocals are added between the lines, not singing the lyrics but offering wordless affirmation until the line "I see my light come shining", where they join in on the lyric. In the background, Weldon Irvine's organ asserts itself, occasionally swirling forward in the soundspace to recall the sounds of the church, of Dylan's classic mid-1960s work with Al Kooper and of Garth Hudson's contributions to The Band's unique sound. During the second verse, Simone's voice grows in intensity and she offers the occasional piano trill as additional texture. With the solid bedrock of Don Alias's drums and Gene Perla's electric bass in place, the other musicians are able to embark on small-scale extemporizations for the rest of the piece, giving a multi-textured and fast-changing sound not unlike that described by Dylan as "wild mercury" (Cott 2006, 208). Unfortunately this is all let down by an unnecessarily violent fade at the song's close. Before listeners have had a chance to savour Simone's final, drawn-out cry of "released", her voice is drowned out and we are into 'I Can't See Nobody'.

Following the Bee Gees cover, we witness Simone's take on 'Just Like Tom Thumb's Blues', a track which originally appeared on Dylan's 1965 album *Highway 61 Revisited*. Sequenced as the penultimate song on Dylan's album, just prior to the epic 'Desolation Row', 'Tom Thumb' introduced a sense of weariness to the proceedings, supported by the feeling of ennui and exhaustion described by the narrator of the lyric and by the cyclically repeating blues deployed by Dylan and his band. That version, however, seems positively upright and alert when compared to Simone's 'Just Like Tom Thumb Blues' (*sic*), which starts with a slow piano riff, wakes up a little with the introduction of Alias's congas, then slouches back into a slow groove with an intimately languid vocal and Shackman's gently weeping guitar (B22, track 8). Mike Butler, who describes Simone's vocal on this track as possessing a "ravaged sexiness" (B22, liner notes), finds her version "more faithful to the subject matter than Dylan's original", especially when she reaches the line "I haven't got the strength to get up and take another shot" (1:13-20). There is certainly a remarkable sense of weariness and powerlessness, which seems to reach its culmination at the point (3:53) where Simone says softly, "Well that's it folks, that's it", a reminder of the kind of phrases she would use at the end of her concert performances. In concert, it often was not "it" as she would hopefully return for an encore. Here, the "encore" is the final, as yet unsung, verse of Dylan's song which keeps the track drifting along for another 45 seconds; when Simone gets to the line "I do believe I've had enough", she sounds completely convincing.

In the context of *To Love Somebody*, however, the Simone–Dylan partnership is not yet finished. The final and longest of the three covers comes with the album's closing track, 'The Times They Are A-Changing' (*sic*), which again places keyboards (Simone's piano and Irvine's organ) centre stage (B22, track 9). Although Dylan's officially released version of the song used acoustic guitar and was therefore easily categorized in the early 1960s as polemical "folk music", Dylan himself switched between guitar and piano even in his early "folk" stage, as can be heard by an alternative version of 'The Times They Are A-Changin'' released on the first of his "Bootleg Series" albums. Simone sings the lyric slowly and dramatically, her voice rising against a backdrop of cymbal washes, piano keyboard runs and stately, funereal organ. She sounds hoarse in places, emoting the line "there's a battle outside and it's *ragin'*" (2:04–2:10) with what sounds like desperation: it is easy to hear the song as a sign of different times to its original moment, a sign of desperation as Simone and others began to realize that the times might not be changing after all. When Irvine takes a church organ-style solo and a bell starts tolling at 3:42, the sense of reverence, sadness and finality is absolute. The verse that follows is the one that begins "The line it is drawn and the curse it is cast"; Simone's drawn-out vocal makes it sound like an ending, and so it proves: the end of the song and album soon follows, its cursed, apocalyptic tone a reflection of the end of a decade of hope. There is a neat symmetry to the move, Simone closing *To Love Somebody* by turning a song of hope and prediction into one of loss and failure after opening the album by turning a somewhat dirge-like song (Leonard Cohen's 'Suzanne') into a bright, joyous event.

'Suzanne'

In discussing Nina Simone's reading of 'Suzanne', it is worth briefly situating the artist within a trio of female performers whose work around the late 1960s and early 1970s provides some fascinating parallels and overlaps. The trio comprises Simone herself, Judy Collins and Roberta Flack. All three had shared roots in classical music. Simone was a child prodigy at the piano and received many years of training that was intended (at least by her and those closest to her) to lead to a career as a classical pianist. For reasons that remained traumatic for her, she was not able to follow this path but she nonetheless made an ultimately successful diversion to popular music and attached herself to a cause that offered to fight against the reasons for her expulsion from the classical music world. Judy Collins (b. 1939) had a similar background in classical piano, training that, due to her race and social status, she was in a better position than Simone to pursue. Nevertheless, she experienced a politicization at a fairly young age that brought about a conversion to folk music, to which she diverted her talents wholeheartedly. Arriving in Greenwich Village in 1961, she became part of the folk crowd described by Simone in her autobiography. Roberta Flack (b. 1939) was, like Simone, a youthful black piano prodigy who went into popular music following a certain amount of formal classical training. All three artists performed a combination of material made up of their own songs and those of others, with the greater proportion being taken up by cover versions. All three had eclectic tastes and covered a wide array of musical styles, including folk, art song, jazz, country, blues, soul, rock and pop. Although the amount of material included in these artists' shared repertoire is small (especially between Collins and Flack) in proportion to their large individual catalogues, it represents an interesting moment in popular music history. The table below gives some indication of how this crossover worked.

Song	Writer	Collins	Simone	Flack
Just Like Tom Thumb's Blues	Dylan	1966[+]	1969	
Pirate Jenny	Brecht/Weill	1966	1964	
Suzanne	Cohen	1966	1969	1973
I Think It's Going To Rain Today	Newman	1966	1969	
Turn! Turn! Turn!	Seeger	1964 1969	1969	
My Father	Collins	1968	1971 1978	
Who Knows Where the Time Goes	Denny	1968	1971	
Hey, That's No Way To Say Goodbye	Cohen	1968		1969
Just Like a Woman	Dylan	1994	1971	1970
If He Changed My Name/I Told Jesus	McGimsey		1962	1969
Do What You Gotta Do	Webb		1968	1970
Let It Be Me	Curtis/ Becaud/ Delanoe		1974 1987	1970
To Love Somebody	Gibb/Gibb		1969	1971

One of the reasons it is worth highlighting these overlaps is the suggestion it provides that, at least in Simone's and Flack's cases, these artists were not necessarily looking to the original sources (Dylan, Cohen, Webb, etc.) for their material but to each other's work. This can be supported by the fact that certain of their versions contain disparities that are inconsistent with the original material but consistent with each other. An example of this can be found in Simone's reading of 'Who Knows Where the Time Goes', which changes the first line of Sandy Denny's original in the same way that Collins's version does. Simone's and Flack's readings of 'Just Like a Woman', meanwhile, make comparable changes to the personal pronouns and include a word ("problems") that did not appear in the original.[5]

Of the three, it tends to be Collins's versions of the songs that maintain the closest lyrical fidelity to the source material. This is perhaps not surprising given the fact that she tends to be the first to record the songs. But it is also noticeable in her late reading of 'Just Like a Woman', which follows Dylan's words exactly and avoids the lyrical improvisations, or permanent alterations, that Simone, Flack and numerous others have added in the intervening years. However, Collins does provide a number of innovations in the music that accompanies her versions. This was a notable development in the album that contained her version of 'Suzanne'. *In My Life* (1966) marked a distinct move from the folk music of her previous five studio albums towards more of an art song approach. This was achieved partly by the inclusion of material such as Richard Peaslee's 'Marat/Sade' and Brecht/Weill's 'Pirate Jenny' (recorded by Nina Simone in 1964), Randy Newman's 'I Think It's Going To Rain Today' (recorded by Simone in 1969), Cohen's 'Suzanne' and 'Dress Rehearsal Rag', and an unusual setting of Bob Dylan's 'Just Like Tom Thumb's Blues' (recorded by Simone in 1969), providing links to music for the theatre and film and to erudite poetry. In addition to this the instrumental backing to the numbers was quite different from that of the folk styles of Collins's earlier career: her version of Richard Farina's 'Hard Lovin' Loser' combined harpsichord with electric blues-rock, for example, while flutes, strings and piano were prominent features of other tracks.

Collins provides a faithful version of 'Suzanne', enunciating the lyric clearly over a descending acoustic guitar figure similar to the one Cohen himself would use in his recording of 1968 (C8, disc 2, track 4; C7, track 1). Taking its place on *In My Life* between 'Pirate Jenny' and Jacques Brel's 'La Colombe', 'Suzanne' is an effective slice of erudite song and a notable debut for Cohen's songwriting skills. It established a performance style – sombre, reflective, slightly monotonous – that would remain fairly constant in numerous future versions of the song. Because the song is wordy and yet subtle (there is a constant shifting of personal pronouns that ensures we are never sure who is singing or to whom) there is a tendency in most renditions not to elaborate on the melody or harmony in order to show fidelity to the material. This has often led to a situation in which, paradoxically, in attempting to master the song, singers have often fallen subject to it.

This subjection is evident to a certain extent in a take of the song recorded by Nina Simone in 1969 but rejected in favour of the (presumably later) version used on *To Love Somebody*. The rejected version (B19, disc 2, track 10) features Simone on piano, marking a different approach to the song than that so far attempted by other singers. As the track progresses, however, Al Shackman's electric guitar gradually dominates and Simone does not sound in complete control of the lyric, with its confusing distribution of personal pronouns. The released version is strikingly different, dominated by Simone's memorable piano arpeggios, a truly innovative addition to the instrumentation of this hitherto exemplary bedsit troubadour anthem (B22, track 1). There is a much brighter tempo and the track seems to make reference to its own recording, sounding like the layered studio construct it no doubt is. In the unreleased version, Simone sounds as if the song is controlling her; here, she has taken complete control. The repetition of certain words, the stretching of notes and use of melisma (the two syllable "mi-ind" from 1:22 to 1:26) all take the song away from its literal meaning. Added interjections (the "yeah" immediately following "mi-ind" at 1:27) suggest that Simone knows she has initiated an irresistible groove and can now add whatever she wishes to it, continue or cease it at whim.

Roberta Flack's version of 'Suzanne' is nearly ten minutes and closes her album *Killing Me Softly* (1973); at the time this accounted for around a quarter of an album (C17, track 8). Appropriately perhaps, given the album it appears on, there is a softness to Flack's version. A constant cymbal ride in the background promises an escalation of the beat that never actually occurs, while a sporadically deployed electric bass marks time rather than developing a rhythm. Only the opening and close of the song seem to suggest freedom. A long introduction on piano provides no clues to the (by this time very familiar) song to come. After the last refrain has been sung, the piano springs to life and the drums follow suit. Strings enter, bringing a sense of soaring drama that had hitherto been absent. Flack improvises wordless vocals, exploring with her voice as the strings waver like sirens. But, seemingly unaware of this promise of freedom, Flack ultimately circles back to the start of the song: "Suzanne takes you down to a place by the river". But it seems as though it is she who has been taken down, imprisoned by the song and unable to escape to the giddy heights discovered by Simone.

My Way

A brilliance similar to her version of 'Suzanne' can be found in Simone's read-ing of 'My Way', a song associated with Frank Sinatra. In anticipation of the material to be discussed in Chapter 4, it is worth noting briefly Simone's and Sinatra's mutual admiration for each other's work and the small but sig-nificant group of songs that both recorded. Interestingly, each has recorded what might be considered the key signature song of the other. Simone is still widely remembered – outside of her more dedicated fan base – for 'My Baby Just Cares For Me', the song that she first recorded in the late 1950s and which has been a notable hit in at least three different eras. Sinatra included a version of the song on his 1969 album *Strangers in the Night*. 'My Way' became Sinatra's signature song in the later stages of his career and a ver-sion by Simone was released in 1971. Other shared repertoire includes Hoagy Carmichael's 'I Get Along Without You Very Well' and Jacques Brel's 'Ne Me Quitte Pas', recorded in French by Simone and in Rod McKuen's translation as 'If You Go Away' by Sinatra. A special group of songs written especially for Sinatra and recorded by Simone – 'For A While', 'The Single Man', 'Lonesome Cities', 'Love's Been Good To Me' – will be considered in the next chapter.

'My Way' originated as a French *chanson* entitled 'Comme d'habitude' ('As Usual'). It was first recorded by Claude François, a popular French singer who co-wrote the song with Gilles Thibaut and Jacques Revaux and included it on his self-titled album in 1967 (C18, track 1). Paul Anka "translated" the lyric into English specifically for Sinatra, changing the main sense of the song's lyrics and its overall message but retaining the melody (C34, track 6). Despite numerous other versions, the song became indelibly associated with Sinatra during the 1970s following his return from "retirement". In a concert recorded for the 1974 album *The Main Event*, he introduced the song by saying, "We will now do the national anthem but you needn't rise". The song is men-tioned a number of times in Will Friedwald's *Sinatra! The Song is You*. Early in the book he writes:

> No popular recording artist has ever been as totally believable
> so much of the time as Sinatra . . . The results come through
> especially clearly in an overtly autobiographical text like 'My
> Way.' Sung by any other interpreter, including the teenage
> idol Paul Anka (who translated it from the original French),
> that 1969 hit would sound like an obnoxious joke. In fact it's a

> deliberate gag in the messy mitts of Sid Vicious and an unin-
> tentional one in the trembling tremolos of Elvis Presley, both
> of whom recorded it (1997, 24).

Readers of Friedwald's book will quickly realize that the author has very little time for contemporary (post rock 'n' roll) popular music, aligning him, to a certain extent, with Sinatra himself, who made a number of disparaging comments in his time about rock, despite recording a number of rock songs. It may be that Friedwald needs to denigrate other song forms, singers and even nations so that he can build up Sinatra's role in author(iz)ing the song:

> Musically, it's an underwhelming composition that contains
> nearly five identical stanzas, each consisting of a string of
> very monotonous four-note phrases . . . Yet the way [Sinatra]
> transforms this unpromising source material takes him
> beyond alchemy and into the realm of sheer magic. Musi-
> cally, it has no more content than most rock and roll, yet
> Sinatra pumps it up with the grandeur of an operatic aria,
> a five-minute exercise in self-indulgence that starts quietly,
> even intimately, and ends enormously (1997, 447).

This is a reasonably convincing account of the song but it rather ignores a number of salient points. Firstly, Friedwald considers this a "translation" of the original French song. However, while the melody has been kept, Anka's words are new ones. To be fair to Friedwald, he does seem to be more inter-ested in the melody and what Sinatra does with it but, as is clear in his refer-ences to the "autobiographical" nature of the song, he also realizes that the words play a crucial role: this really *is* Sinatra looking back on his life, a mes-sage from him to us. Given the centrality of the words, it seems clear that we cannot make a comparison with the French version without taking account of *what the latter is saying*. It is a song about routine, about mundanity, in which every negative thing repeats itself "as usual". This is a radically differ-ent message to that of 'My Way', a song about escaping the usual and being an individual. Furthermore, there is the issue of agency. 'Comme d'habitude' presents us with a narrator completely at the mercy of fate and the will of the other, while 'My Way' provides a battler against fate's whims, someone whom fate has made stronger and who is able to "stand tall" and face society.

In this sense, 'Comme d'habitude' can be connected to the *chanson* tradition and to other fatalistic song forms such as *fado* and country. A comparison of the songs leads us to the representation of mastery and submission. While the narrator of 'Comme d'habitude' "plays at pretending" and submits to the domination of the other ("I will wait for you", he sings), the narrator of 'My Way' dominates, looking down on the kind of man "who kneels". Gender, of course, is crucial here. "What is a man?" Sinatra asks. Clearly one who can claim all the acts and the agency that 'My Way' boasts, one who can master himself, others and fate itself. For Friedwald, this mastery extends to Sinatra himself, the only man who can take such paltry (feminine?) material and conjure "sheer magic" from it with his massive voice/ phallus, shatter its "intimacy" with his "enormity". François, meanwhile, is left whining and weeping into his coffee, not man enough to take control of his life or his woman. We do not know from Friedwald's account whether he is familiar with the French lyrics but it does not require too much speculation, given what he does say about "French songs" and "kiddie-pop", to interpret his account of 'My Way' as a masculine response to a feminine problem.

The droning rhythm and repetition of the melody – which Friedwald finds typical of "French songs" (1997, 446) – seems entirely suited to the lyrical preoccupations of 'Comme d'habitude', and François's version highlights this by introducing difference at the climax of the song, perhaps signifying anger finally boiling over, an escape from submission, a warning note, the hint of violence (perhaps, in this light, Sinatra merely finishes what François has initiated). What Friedwald does not ask is why Paul Anka kept the melody of the French song and lost the words. Is it possible that Anka wished to transfer the "monotony" of the melody to his account of the winner who rises above the mundane, setting in motion a dialectic between word and melody? In this sense, the song can be read as an escape from *d'habitude* and the habitus from which it draws its sense of itself and its self-difference: in other words, it comes to be about creativity.

This is the manner in which Nina Simone approaches 'My Way', the closing track of *Here Comes the Sun* (B22, track 17). Her version allows us to play Friedwald at his own game, as Mike Butler seems to do when he offers the following summary of the performance:

> Is this the definitive My Way? Nina Simone, an individual-
> ist if ever there was one, is free from the self-deception that

disqualifies most of the field. Which leaves Frank Sinatra and Sid Vicious. The present version generates excitement from the off: bongos double the tempo as Nina takes her first note; strings swell in rising excitement; harpsichord and harp rip along, adding period charm. Nina is exultant as she swoops and dives over the hypnotic Latin beat. Frank sounds doleful in comparison, as if he can't wait for the final curtain, and Sid is just plain silly. There's no competition, really (B22, liner notes).

A number of questions immediately arise from this. What does it mean to give a definitive version? What does it mean to say that someone really gets to what the song was about? How might this differ with songs thought of as songs (the products of songwriters) rather than as original performances? In pop, the songwriter and the original performer are sometimes the same: in rock, almost invariably. To say someone has found something fundamental in the song *qua* song is to say they gave a proper interpretation to the piece; to say someone gets to the fundamental in a song that was already a sup-posedly definitive performance seems less straightforward. This does not, of course, stop music fans – including critics and other musicians – from doing so.

Mike Butler's question as to whether Nina Simone's version of 'My Way' is the definitive one might seem absurd unless viewed through the fantasy of authenticity. How can a song about doing it *my way* have a definitive version? And is a "definitive" version the same as an "authoritative" version? These are different words with different meanings and yet they are often used synony-mously in qualitative accounts of culture. While a dictionary may list many definitions of a word, we are unlikely to hear someone say that a version of a song is *a* definitive version (among others); it is invariably *the* definitive version, making it synonymous with the authoritative version. But isn't 'My Way' precisely about not taking part in something that can be defined, essen-tialized or authorized? Isn't it, rather, about individualism and individual per-spective? Does 'My Way' actually gesture towards a nascent identity politics? We certainly witness such a possibility in the versions by Nina Simone and Sid Vicious. They sing it *their way* and their way is entirely fitting *for them*. Only the illusion created by the fantasy of authenticity allows one of them to be definitive. We are talking, then, of an ideological battle for authenticity, authorship and authority rather than a cool judgement on aesthetics and style. And while this may seem to lead us into the quagmire of relativism, the fantasy of authentication tends to stop us long before we sink too far, allowing us, perhaps, to declare a victor.

The conversation Nina Simone has with 'My Way' is, as Butler intimates, a fascinating one, with the artist in complete control of her material. In addition to the features Butler mentions – harp, harpsichord, "Latin" beat – it is hard not to be surprised by the transition from one stanza to the next. Where Sinatra's version had finished each section on a decisive note, Simone's immediately completes the final line (each "my way") with twelve quick keyboard stabs which work both to emphasize the line and to give a sense of climax to each verse. As a sense of ambiguity descends – will the song end here? – Simone's right hand picks a bright ascending figure out of each "final" chord and leads us into the next verse. Each verse brings more with it musically – extra percussion, electric bass, strings – leading to a situation where, at each demise and resurrection, there is an overwhelming sense of excess. Indeed, for a song already so steeped in excess in Sinatra's versions – especially his live performances – it seems as if Simone is trying to deliberately exceed The Voice himself.

Simone makes few changes to the lyric – "shy way" becomes "sly way", "friend" is changed to "friends", "spit" corrected to "spat" – and none to the sequence of the song. This is in marked contrast to her version of Dylan's 'Just Like A Woman' from the same album, where she places a chorus before the first verse, misses one whole verse out and, crucially, plays around with the problematic personal pronouns of the song. She does, however, add melisma and occasional interjections to the words, giving a sense of control over the material and the groove of the song (a groove her version invents, of course: who could have thought of this as a groovy song before? Certainly not "monotonous" Claude François, nor Sinatra/Friedwald). At the start of the second verse a stretched "ye-es" (0:46–0:47) provides a vocal accompaniment to the keyboard's lead-in, providing both musical and linguistic transition ("yes, regrets . . .": *of course I've had them but that's not what's important now*). At the very end of the last verse, the point where Sinatra's version would be building to its climax ("The record shows/I took the blows/And did it/My/Way"), Simone adds melisma to the final "way", stretching it to four syllables, then lets it fade into the rising strings which now take over from the vocal – there is no repetition (reassertion) of the final line. We are only 3:26 into the song when Simone's vocal dies away. But she and the other musicians are not finished; fully aware she has set up an irresistible groove (Butler says "hypnotic": "infectious" seems nearer the mark[6]), she lets the orchestra ride the song out for another minute and a half. Strings soar, swoop, hover, dive; a cymbal taps out a jazzy rhythm to add to the melange; Simone indulges herself on the piano as if she has deserved it; the strings grow in crescendo; soulful backing vocals join in; and it all fades out far too soon. It is a spectacular way to close an album and it seems no coincidence that it is placed at the end of *Here Comes the Sun*, just as Sinatra would come to place the song at the climax of his live shows. Indeed, one could argue that Simone has discovered and disseminated the eventual possibilities of 'My Way' long before we get to hear them on *The Main Event*. What is the "main event" referred to in the title of that album? Is it to Frank Sinatra as the headline act? In which case, is his finale of 'My Way' the main event of this main event? If so, it seems that Simone has beaten him at his own game.

Simone as Site, Sight and Sound: Filmed Performance

Arguably the most complete and enjoyable way of experiencing the various types of possession discussed in this chapter comes from viewing Nina Simone in live performance. This is now only possible via video recordings, of which, thankfully, there are some fine extant examples. The Jazz Icons DVD released by Naxos in 2008 contains impressive performances from the 1960s, including the 1965 Dutch TV broadcast that has already been discussed in terms of its political programme. It is worth saying a little more about these performances, and the others included in the Jazz Icons collection, as a way of bringing together and concluding the various discussions of possession in this chapter.

Highlights of the Dutch set include the moment during the opening 'Brown Baby' when, having arrived at the lyric about living "by the justice code" and walking down "freedom's road", Simone swoops into falsetto to deliver the last two words. While some falsetto had been used in the version included on *At the Village Gate*, it had not been at this point and we do not get to see her face as we do on the DVD; singing "freedom road" her features crease into a frown, no doubt due to the effort to switch vocal register but readable as representing the pain involved in the struggle to reach that road. The version of 'Four Women', meanwhile, is notable for the way in which Simone adopts a distinct voice and body language for each of the women, moving from narrator to actor as she sways seductively to Sweet Thing's tale and fixing the audience with her angriest look when it comes to the turn of Peaches. The most startling moment of possession comes during 'Hollis Brown', where Simone appears to completely enter the story and to be channelling it from "somewhere in the distance" that the lyric refers to. As Rob Bowman notes, she is "seemingly possessed, as if in a trance", only snapping out of it at the sound of the crowd's applause (F5, liner notes). Simone also shows her ability to reinvent her own material, adding new phrasing and scat singing to her performance of 'Mississippi Goddam' in a manner that asserts her mastery of jazz idioms (ibid.).

The second live set included in the Jazz Icons DVD is a British television broadcast from 1968. It offers a fine version of 'Ain't Got No / I Got Life' which offers visual proof of the assertion of physicality discussed earlier in this chapter. Bowman, who is dismissive of the original version of the song in the musical *Hair!*, argues that "if proof were ever needed that meaning in music is ultimately determined in performance, Simone's version of 'Ain't Got No/I Got Life' would suffice" (F5, liner notes). On 'Backlash Blues', Simone stabs at the piano, sways her upper body to the rhythm and even leaps up from her stool in time to the music, seemingly seized by the spirit of the song and yet never losing the impression that she is in complete control of music, band, material and audience. Another aspect of possession-as-ownership that can be noted here is the practice of self-naming. While it was argued in the last chapter that we should not necessarily confuse the characters in a song such as 'Four Women' with the artist herself, it is nevertheless the case that Simone did often conflate character and narrator, whether through the changing of personal pronouns (as in 'Just Like A Woman') or the use of her own name or those of people close to her. Such self-naming can be found as far back as 'Nobody' on *Broadway-Blues-Ballads* and would become increasingly prevalent in the later stages of Simone's career, as discussed in the next chapter. An example of the naming of others can be found in the insertion of her brother Carrol's name into 'Just Like Tom Thumb Blues' and, again, in numerous late performances. Both types of naming occur in the live performance of 'Backlash Blues', as Simone narrates how Langston Hughes told her to "tell them exactly where it's at". By following his instructions, and telling her audience about it, Simone becomes both the medium through which Hughes's posthumous voice may send its message and a self-reflexive chronicler of her own life, times and work.

The sense of Simone as medium is further emphasized in the short but intense version of 'I Put a Spell on You' included in the British broadcast. Dressed in an African headdress, Simone frowns towards some point between her piano and the television camera, intoning Hawkins's lyric in what initially amounts to a monotone. Improvising on the original lyric, Simone adds, "I went to Alabama and I got me some mojo dust and I put a spell on you". Lifting her left hand to her face as if not completely in control of her body, she then utters a set of sounds that are even more unintelligible than those on her studio recording of the song, before bringing the song to a close after only a minute and a half. Following up with "the things that we think will please you the most", Simone then offers a version of 'Don't Let Me Be Misunderstood', which, she notes, had been a hit for The Animals in Britain. It is fairly well known that Simone had been unhappy with the success the British group had had with a song she considered hers and her ironic introduction of it here as a "request", along with the understated delivery of the song, could be considered a repossession of the song in front of British witnesses.

Conclusion

In this chapter, I have considered some of the ways in which Nina Simone's art privileges various notions of possession. Performances were chosen that emphasize physical embodiment, either through the directly embodied address of the Blues Queen or the more tangled (dis)embodiment made possible via multiple narrative voices. Simone's religious background was highlighted once more, along with her lifelong interest in the transformative, affective power of religious and ritual practices. As we saw, the conflation of practices derived from the Southern Church with those associated with Africa and the Caribbean, while perhaps not showing fidelity to any one set of beliefs, nevertheless continuously asserted faith in the power of turning-on, coming-through, transporting and transforming. What coherence could be found in the "Church of Nina" was brought into existence both through these possessive practices and through the convincing ownership of other artists' material. My claims concerning Simone's "victory" in owning certain material will not convince everyone. Nevertheless, it is not a wild claim to suggest that the process of "Simone-ization" recognized early in the artist's career – in which her versions were heard to possess distinctive qualities – was one that she maintained at a consistently high level. In the chapter that follows, I will consider some later appropriations and suggest that the conversation that Simone has with them becomes ever more personal, with "Simone-ization" becoming not just a stylistic appropriation but a way in which the artist uses other people's song texts to tell her own story.

4 Lateness

Introduction

Nina Simone's body of work is one in which issues of musical style, categorization and virtuosity are played out alongside those of social history, politics and biography in fascinating ways. The biographical aspects of Simone's work are characterized by the interplay of innocence and experience, a feature which becomes more notable as one follows Simone through her entire career. As with many performers, we find in Simone's mature work a greater emphasis on life experience, perhaps not surprising given that there are more years to look back on, not to mention the sense in which a commercial, if not artistic, peak has been passed. More than this, however, I believe that there is a feeling of lateness to much of Simone's work, and not only that produced late in her career; while there is certainly a marked increase in nostalgic memory work during the later years, the concept of a "late voice" is one which can be retroactively read into even some of Simone's earliest work (Elliott 2008a: 251–87). Lateness, in the sense in which I am using it here, is a concept exemplified by Simone's work but which extends to a broad range of modern (post mid-twentieth-century) popular musics. It refers to five primary issues: chronology (the stage in an artist's career); the vocal act (the ability to convincingly portray experience); afterlife (posthumous careers made possible by phonography); retrospection (how voices "look back" or anticipate looking back); and the writing of age, experience, lateness and loss into song texts.

Classical musicology has a well-established history of associating particular stylistic characteristics to periods in the lives of composers, while theorizations of lateness and late style in music (Adorno 2002; Said 2005; Spitzer 2006) have invariably privileged classical music. Although popular music has not received comparable treatment, pop artists, as performers in the public eye, offer a privileged site for the witnessing and analysis of ageing and its mediation. Supplementing theorizations of the ways that lived experience mixes with "lettered experience", "learned experience" and "the experience of images" in art and literature (Agacinski 2003, 56–7), a more music-based analysis allows us to posit the concept of "sounded experience" (Elliott 2010: 126–30), a term intended to describe how music reflects upon and helps to mediate life experience over extended periods of time (indeed, over lifetimes).

Nina Simone's Lateness

For Russell Berman (2004), Nina Simone's refusal of categorization is connected to an individualism that takes off from where collective politics ends or fails. For Ashley Kahn, however, it is the refusal itself which is political: "Forever binding music and message, Simone ultimately saw her defiance of category – social, racial, musical – as an intrinsic part of her mission of self-affirmation and protest" (B10, liner notes). This would seem to tie in with Simone's own views; in her autobiography she claimed, "For black musicians the result of the sixties was exile to dance music and the old black ghettoes of jazz and blues" (Simone and Cleary 2003, 136). While many have suggested that black music has sought to move on to new styles whenever its previous innovations have been co-opted by the white mainstream, a process that leads to a recurrent black creativity in popular music, Simone seems to find an attachment to black music occasionally regressive rather than progressive. And while the developments in black soul, jazz, blues and funk are arguably manifestations of a range of political aesthetics – Berman's point – Simone would seem to suggest that her politics resides in her ability to take on the pop mainstream and do it her way. This does appear at odds with her oft-recorded advocacy of black separatism over assimilation, and of militancy over diplomacy, but these are all aspects of what Kahn calls her "enduring enigma" (B10, liner notes). In an overview of Simone's work for RCA, Stuart Nicholson suggests that the mixture of militant protest material with lightweight pop fare was a way for her to smuggle the former material past the record company executives responsible for releasing her albums (B20, liner notes). This may well be true to a certain extent but it would be wrong to assume that Simone was only interested in serious or protest music and only included pop material to please others. There is a tendency for critics, biographers and other commentators to assume that because *they* do not consider certain material of high quality, there must have been some motive in Simone's choice of the material other than aesthetic pleasure. There are, however, numerous examples of concert performances where Simone showed very little concern about others' desires and yet still performed mainstream pop songs that had seemingly little to do with "the cause". It is worth recalling Robin Kelley's point (discussed in Chapter 2) that, while issues of class, race, gender and other aspects of identity politics are vital when discussing popular culture, this should not be to the exclusion of aesthetic or other types of pleasure. I would argue that it is with such issues in mind – and in particular the bittersweet pleasures of memory, nostalgia and unresolved yearning – that we should approach Nina Simone's late voice.

As for teleology, which is always at least implied in any discussion of lateness, Kahn (B10, liner notes) warns against seeing stylistic progression from one point of Simone's career to another, stressing rather an expansion of the repertoire with the old numbers still played, performed, recorded, updated. Indeed, in a manner analogous to the way Ajay Heble (2000, 93) highlights Paul Robeson's changing improvisations of the lyrics to 'Ol' Man River' over the years to reflect the presence of black resistance to the white mainstream, it is worth noting the way Nina Simone continued to improvise on the lyrics of 'Mississippi Goddam' late in her career to work in references to Ronald Reagan, Margaret Thatcher, Jesse Jackson and Michael Jackson amongst others. The song has this possibility built into its structure so that, even in its original form – let us call this the version we witness on *In Concert* (1964) – the final payoff involves the introduction of new terms ("Alabama", for example) into the "Mississippi" placeholder ("Everybody knows about _____"). However, while I agree with Kahn that Simone's repertoire was one that defied neat chronology, I want to suggest here that a distinctive "late voice" can be identified, one that is compatible with Berman's observations about Simone's sentimentalism and with accounts – including Simone's own – of the singer's increasing disillusionment over the failure of the civil rights movement. Ron Eyerman describes this "failure" as follows:

> The 1960s appeared differently to whites and blacks. Whites tend to remember the sixties as filled with political and cultural confrontation, where young college students protested against the war in Vietnam, where a sexual revolution altered the boundaries of what was normal and acceptable, and where feminism changed the way Americans looked at gender, marriage and family life. . . . Blacks, especially those influenced by cultural nationalism, remember something different. Here the period tends to be viewed through a

> perceived defeat of the civil rights movement, the failure to
> either achieve its goals of inclusion or to speak to the specific
> needs of urban blacks. The failure, in other words, of the pro-
> gressive narrative (2001, 191).

The loss of the ideals of the movement followed the loss of so many individuals associated with it. Nina Simone was painfully aware of these losses. In her
Westbury performance three nights after the assassination of Martin Luther
King, she used three songs to comment on the event. The first of these, 'Sunday in Savannah', was presented as a song of comfort for those who had
come to the concert. The second was Gene Taylor's 'Why? (The King Of Love
Is Dead)'. Midway through, Simone paused to reflect on the loss of King and
others: "Lorraine Hansberry left us . . . and then Langston Hughes left us, Coltrane left us, Otis Redding left us. Who can go on? Do you realize how many
we have lost? . . . We can't afford any more losses. . . . They're shooting us
down one by one." The third song was the defiant 'Mississippi Goddam', tailored to the particular events of three days before.[1]

Simone's mourning of King connects to a wider awareness of the loss of
political projects and lost utopias (Elliott 2008a). While Simone had tended
to align herself more with the militant demands of Malcolm X, Stokely Carmichael and Eldridge Cleaver than the utopian dreams of King, and while
she could still interject militant demands into renditions of 'Mississippi Goddam' such as the one performed in the wake of King's assassination ("I ain't
about to be nonviolent honey!" she shouts at one point), and even as she was
writing and recording a track called 'Revolution' (which can be heard as an
answer-song to John Lennon's critically mauled song of the same name), she
had an increasing sense that it was all for nothing. In a kind of reverse mirror
stage, the illusion of being a whole person, of having an important role to
play in the Symbolic Order, slowly started to shatter:

> I didn't suddenly wake up one morning feeling dissatisfied.
> These feelings just became more and more intense, until by
> the time the sixties ended I'd look in the mirror and see two
> faces, knowing that on the one hand I loved being black and
> being a woman, and that on the other it was my colour and
> sex which had fucked me up in the first place (Simone and
> Cleary 2003, 118).

She continues:

> The days when revolution really had seemed possible were
> gone forever. I watched the survivors run for cover in com-
> munity and academic programmes and felt betrayed, partly
> by our own leaders but mostly by white America. And I felt
> disgusted by my own innocence. I had presumed we could
> change the world and had run down a dead-end street leav-
> ing my career, child and husband way behind, neglected.
> Optimists talked about the advances we had made, but all I
> saw were lost opportunities (Simone and Cleary 2003, 118).

Weighed down by the burden of knowledge and the realization that the
promised event had not materialized, Simone attempted to "calm the passion of being" (Alain Badiou's phrase [2005, 294]) by moving away from the
USA and withdrawing from the public eye. Her "disappearance" was such
that, in an obituary for the singer in 2003, Dave Marsh felt able to write that
"Nina Simone hadn't made an important record or written a well-known
song since the early 1970s, so in a sense her absence will not be widely felt"
(preface to Simone and Cleary 2003, vi). I would dispute the accuracy of this
statement, not least because it is unclear for whom Marsh was speaking. As
Mark Anthony Neal (2003) points out, and as will be discussed in the next
chapter, Simone continued to matter a great deal to African Americans during her years of exile. Nevertheless, it is certainly true that Simone's position
in the public eye moved from one based on the present to one based on past
triumphs.

The notion of the artist as "a shadow of their former self", or even a pastiche of their former self, is one of the ways in which loss is inscribed into the
discourse of popular music's teleology, albeit a teleology described less as a
move towards something than as a move away. Rather than dwelling here
on the level (or lack) of acceptance of ageing in popular music discourse, I
wish to note how a move may often be seen to be made from early innova-
tion to later memory work. This memory work may result in the often-seen
re-presentation of an artist as a living repository of past hits ("golden oldies")
but may also lead to the creation of a quite new persona.

Richard Leppert's and George Lipsitz's (1990) "Age, the Body and Experience in the Music of Hank Williams" provides a useful way of theorizing how

Williams was able to convincingly speak to an audience undergoing profound changes in identity politics. Highlighting his broad appeal to whites and blacks, his "standpoint as a worker and an ordinary citizen", his resistance to "the dominant oedipal narrative", and his foregrounding of "existential despair in an age of exuberant and uncritical 'progress'", the authors argue that Williams's success resulted from an ability to combine an articulation of age and experience while maintaining an image of vulnerability. In constructing their argument, Leppert and Lipsitz emphasize the way that Williams "feminized" his male narratives via his vocal style. Williams's emphasis on unrequited love allowed an articulation of failure that connects to this book's main subject:

> By emphasizing a love that is never responded to, as opposed to a love that once was but is now lost, unrequited love songs fundamentally account for an equally defeating – if not necessarily worse – sort of failure: the inability to find love in the first place, to love but not be loved in return, to be rejected. It is in songs of unrequited love that the work of Hank Williams approaches black music most directly, and where it crosses gender lines into emotional ground more commonly occupied by women, and notably by women who are black (e.g. Billie Holiday, Nina Simone). As Billie Holiday, dying, gravel-voiced, movingly – and pathetically – sang in 'Glad to be Unhappy', one of her last recorded songs, when someone you adore fails to love you back, "It's a pleasure to be sad" (Leppert and Lipsitz 1990, 269).

Following their mention of the "dying" Billie Holiday's articulation of the pleasure of unrequited love, Leppert and Lipsitz reference Nina Simone's rendition of 'He Needs Me' from her debut album. It is intriguing to wonder how the experiences of the twenty-five-year-old Simone can be compared to those of the "dying" Holiday. This is not a question of the wider historical context – Holiday's last recordings and Simone's first are contemporaneous and comparison between the material they are performing both relevant and illuminating – but of the context in which the material is presented in terms of the individual's history. In other words, it is a question of biography again.[2]

Leppert and Lipsitz argue that Hank Williams was able to project a voice of experience from an early age partly through the use of techniques such as the vocal "tear" and partly through his own considerable experience. What I want to think of as Williams's, Holiday's, Simone's or others' late voice is both a reflection of this reality and a fantasy conjured by a vocal act. Young singers can and do sing effective songs of loss, which could, in this light, be reduced to particular musical patterns, instrumental and vocal techniques (witness, for example, Nina Simone's achingly melancholic reading of 'Cotton Eyed Joe' on the 1960 album *At Town Hall* or any of the laments on her debut album). Similarly their affect could be reduced to particular effects on the listener caused by particular sound combinations which might be isolated and "proved" effective or otherwise. But we should also keep in mind the *learnt* nature of these effects and consider that if the recognition of musical patterns relating to loss is always learnt – if, in other words, there are no musical universals – then age, biography and experience are always already implicated into the perception of music.

The abuse-scarred voices of Williams and Holiday attested to the possibility of a late voice attained early; Nina Simone and Frank Sinatra, on the other hand, provide examples of artists who, though having sung numerous songs of loss and experience early in their careers, came to be associated with late voices tailored to their particular circumstances. In Sinatra's case, from the late 1950s onwards, this involved the dialectics of mastery and submission, middle-aged suavity and vulnerability; in the case of Simone, from the mid-1970s onwards, it involved a re-appropriation of the kind of experienced-but-vulnerable voice that Leppert and Lipsitz attribute to Williams. To what extent these voices spoke to listeners no doubt depends to a great extent on the amount of knowledge listeners had of the artists. The numerous music lovers for whom Nina Simone remains the voice and piano of 'My Baby Just Cares For Me' would not necessarily recognize any of what I am going to suggest about her later yearning and disappointment. There will be other listeners for whom the late voice works as an articulation of a life whose story they know fairly well. Sinatra's and Simone's are lives publicly lived, and if Simone's later years are less well-known, no one who has read her autobiography or seen *La Légende* is likely to hear her late music without endowing it with a powerful sense of loss. But there is another connection between the personal and the public as well, the process described by Eyerman and Jamison (1998) where "movement artists" act as representatives of collective traumas.

'Who Knows Where the Time Goes'

Before looking at the Sinatra songs appropriated by Nina Simone later in her career, I wish to reflect on some recordings from the 1970s. The first is Simone's reading of Sandy Denny's 'Who Knows Where the Time Goes', released by Simone on *Black Gold* (1970), a live album recorded during a New York concert in October 1969. I wish to consider this song in light of its preoccupation with the late voice, in particular the way the late voice can refer both to an actual voice of experience and to a predictive process that voices experience as future anteriority. Simone was only thirty-six when she recorded the song but she manages to pour a lifetime's experience into her rendition. What is perhaps more remarkable is the sense of experience already extant in the original version of the song by the young Sandy Denny (b. 1947). Denny first recorded the song with the Strawbs in 1967, when she was twenty, and again two years later with Fairport Convention (on the album *Unhalfbricking*). Fairport's version opens with the narrator gazing "across the evening sky" at the birds departing for the winter and wondering how they know "it's time for them to go" (C15, track 6). Having set a pastoral scene of herself dreaming before the winter fire, Denny moves into the song's meditative refrain, the repeated line "Who knows where the time goes?" She lingers on the second "goes", running it over several resolution bars and musically connecting with bandmate Richard Thompson's bubbling guitar. As Thompson takes the baton, Denny's voice fades with her dwindling breath, a reminder of time's inexorable march. A second verse likens the departure of "fickle friends" to the birds in the first verse. Again, the singer remains rooted to the spot, with "no thought of leaving" and no fear in the passing of time and companionship; again, the refrain sings otherwise, its unanswerable question swept downstream by the music's relentless current. The third and final verse suggests the singer has a lover near and that it is their presence that banishes the fear of time, along with the knowledge that the birds will return in spring. In each verse, a claim is made ("I have no thought of time", "I do not count the time", "I do not fear the time") which seems to be disputed by the refrain.

Should we hear the song as one of innocence or experience? Perhaps it is both. On the one hand, it is a song of youthful wonder; experience may not only be unnecessary but it may be the very lack of experience that can command such wonder. The question posed by the young Sandy Denny is a more sophisticated version of the child's endless "Why . . . ?", of a seemingly infinite fascination with the world. On the other hand, the sense of childhood's end, of being abandoned by "fickle friends" and loss of what was taken for granted is palpable. Experience hardens the dreamer and warns that, as the cycle of the seasons turns, so loss will be recurrent on the journey through life. One thus steels oneself against inevitable loss: "I have no fear of time" builds a façade of confidence that the subsequent music cannot support. But just as importantly, the words are time*less* and this no doubt accounts for the number of cover versions of the song and of its ability to mean different things at different stages of its performers' and audiences' lives.

The late voice, when applied to this song, is both a voice arrived at – a voice of time, experience and loss – and a future anterior speech act, an enquiry made by a youthful voice in anticipation of experience it does not yet possess. This may be about technique, the calculated donning of a particular vocal mask. It may be effective acting, the successful passing on of an imaginary self-image to a credulous other. It may be the successful attachment of an enquiry to a place outside the immediate situation, a moment or event that allows the artist to found a truth not yet articulated to her peers (Adorno 2002; Said 2005). It is a moment that stops time, reflects it and sets it back on a different track.

Paradoxical as this future anteriority might seem, it is something we recognize when we use phrases such as "wise beyond her years". It is interesting to compare Denny's song with 'Meet on the Ledge', a song written by bandmate Richard Thompson and recorded by Fairport Convention the same year. Thompson was nineteen when he wrote this reflection on lost friends. 'Meet on the Ledge' seems far less ambiguous a song about loss than does 'Who Knows . . .', being genuinely a song of looking back. Connecting to the points I make here about future anteriority, Ashley Hutchings describes Thompson's song as "the boy genius displaying his powers with an assurance well beyond his years. 'Meet on The Ledge' has no right to come from such a green pen, and those soaring solos have no right to come from such young fingers" (C14, liner notes).[3]

It is possible that Nina Simone heard 'Who Knows Where the Time Goes' on Judy Collins's album of the same name (1968), given that she attempted to record Collins's song 'My Father' not long after recording Denny's song.

Like Collins, she changes the first line to "Across the morning sky", thus suggesting a paradox: if Denny's version was a song of innocence, why did it start in the evening? Surely this "morning sky" version gets closer to the wide-eyed wonder of the innocent? However, Simone offers a preamble to the song that emphasizes its reflective aspect and makes it clear that she reads the song as one of experience:

> Let's see what we can do with this lovely, lovely thing that goes past all racial conflict and all kinds of conflict. It is a reflective tune and some time in your life you will have occasion to say "What is this thing called time? You know, what is that?" . . . [T]ime is a dictator, as we know it: where does it go? What does it do? Most of all, is it alive? Is it a thing that we cannot touch and is it alive? And then one day you look in the mirror – how old – and you say, "Where did the time go?" We leave you with that one (B7).

Where Denny's version of the song with Fairport Convention drew much of its affect from its stately pace, Simone's derives its power from its use of silence, beginning with the introduction. She speaks very softly, creating an intimacy that invites her audience to start to think about time. Such intimacy can cause an awareness of time's passing that, contrary to the assertion in Denny's lyric, brings about fear. Eva Hoffman, describing the "chronophobia" she experienced as a child, recalls reading in the silence of her room and "listening to the clock . . . aware that each tick-tock was irreversible, and that the stealing of time, second by second, would never stop" (2011, 1). On the other hand, an imposed silence can encourage us to turn to our memory in order to negotiate sensory confusion. As Pierre Nora writes in regard to official silences, "the observance of a commemorative minute of silence, which might seem to be a strictly symbolic act, disrupts time, thus concentrating memory" (1996, 14). As both Nora and Hoffman observe, it is time that allows us to think about time: "the need for reflection, for making sense of our transient condition, is time's paradoxical gift to us, and possibly the best consolation for its ultimate power" (Hoffman 2011, 11).

Although 'Who Knows Where the Time Goes' engages with chronophobia (albeit one that the narrator herself denies), it is arguably more concerned with reflection. This is true for the versions by Denny, Collins and Simone;

what Simone's version may be said to add is a sense of "dislocation" that "exacerbates the consciousness of time" (Hoffman 2011, 4). This results from the silence and stillness at the heart of Simone's rendition, a silence which seems to be, paradoxically, even louder on record because of the listener's knowledge that they are listening to a live recording. The "silence" of the concert hall is not really that silent, as John Cage and others proved long ago, and the addition of audience, equipment and other background noise adds layers of sound against which the fragility of Simone's stark performance is forced to compete. Initially backed only by a gently strummed acoustic guitar, she slowly sings the first two verses and refrains before taking a brief yet quietly virtuosic piano solo. The sense of reverie is enhanced when, in the first verse, she stretches the word "dreaming" (3:02–3:09) and uses melisma to make the word flutter slightly above the melody, as if relocating the song itself to a space of dreaming and contemplation. During the second verse soft percussion enters (4:15 onwards), a single, steady beat that, at 60 bpm, echoes the ticking of a clock and serves as a reminder of the passing of time. For the third verse the piano is silent again and Weldon Irvine's organ shimmers ghost-like in the background. The overall impression is one of peaceful, thoughtful reflection and a yearning devoid of any bitterness (it "goes past . . . all kinds of conflict"). This makes what happens next all the more surprising. Before the final "goes" has disappeared the band comes crashing in, organ, electric guitar and percussion providing what is presumably a climax to the show ("we leave you with that one"). It is a shocking moment, jolting us from our reverie. Time seemed to have stood still, we let it go by, not knowing where it went, unworried until the band returned like a superego telling us to move on from our fantasy. It is both part of the masquerade – the abrupt climax to the show – and brutally honest, suggesting that experience can be a shattering process as much as the gradual one Simone narrates in her introduction. It might also be likened to an alarm clock recalling dreamers to the demands of the day.

Interestingly, when including 'Who Knows Where the Time Goes' on the box set *To Be Free*, the producers chose to remove both Simone's introduction and the band's conclusion, allowing it to retain its sense of reverie and to be considered as a song outside the context of the concert, while also making it more directly comparable to versions by Denny and Collins. Mike Butler's description of the performance as "a dream encounter between Nina and Sandy Denny" (B7, liner notes) seems entirely apt, even if it is not clear whose dream Butler is referring to. "Dream" captures something of the ethereal, uncanny otherness of this magisterial performance, while "meeting" recognizes that Simone's version does not replace, better or reinvent Denny's, but rather encounters it in a timeless and liminal space. Rarely has the fragility of time, space and existence been caught so effectively on tape.

'Stars'

If 'Who Knows Where the Time Goes' allows us to connect lateness to the perception of time and experience within song texts, it is Simone's remarkable performance of a song by another young female singer-songwriter that allows us to connect time and experience with biography. 'Stars' was recorded by its writer Janis Ian in 1972, when she was twenty-one, and became the title track of her first mature album for CBS in 1974. Ian had found fleeting fame at an early age after recording the controversial 'Society's Child' in 1965 when she was fourteen. The song, which described an interracial love affair, made as many enemies for Ian, when it gained wider exposure two years later, as 'Mississippi Goddam' had for Nina Simone.[4] Ian followed her brush with success by recording four albums for Victor that, in the artist's own words, "did nothing but waste vinyl" (C22, liner notes). Not wishing to be a one-hit wonder, Ian spent several years working on sound engineering, vocal phrasing ("breathing Billie Holiday and Edith Piaf" [ibid.]), honing her songwriting skills and attempting to overcome the confusion of early success. Reflecting on the period three decades later, she wrote:

> Having a monumental hit at 14 leaves you feeling like a fake; you know your talent enabled you to write a few really good songs, but you don't know how you did it. You're completely dependent on talent and chance, and those are not enough to see you through a career. So I listened to every great songwriter I could find, from Dylan to Johnny Mercer. And I read, omnivorously, from Rimbaud to Ray Bradbury, trying to develop a sense of style (ibid.).

That style had clearly been developed by the time Ian came to write and record 'Stars', a song which develops its narrative over several long and quite complex stanzas while repeatedly returning to the refrain "Stars, they come and go / they come fast they come slow / they go like the last light of the sun all in a blaze". The "stars" theme, the multiple internal rhymes and the solo acoustic guitar accompaniment bear certain resemblances to Don McLean's 'Vincent', a song that Ian claims influenced the writing of 'Stars'. However, while McLean limited his cosmic reference to the "starry starry night" in which Vincent's tragic story was played out, Ian is more concerned with celebrity. The verses of 'Stars' describe those who "live their lives in sad cafes and music halls", dealing with issues of age, appearance and public attention. A verse about those who become famous when young and are then told that they have "had their day" is easy to read as having autobiographical content for Ian and while the sadness of "living with a name you never owned" could apply to anyone whose public fame relies on the culture industry, it might well be another autobiographical confession. Ian also considers those who attained fame when older and who seem to be tougher and better able to deal with its consequences: "perhaps they have a soul they're not afraid to bear / or perhaps there's nothing there". Finally, towards the end of her long (7:13) song, Ian acknowledges the navel-gazing aspect of her ruminations and offers her listeners some solace: "if you don't lose patience with my fumbling around / I'll come up singing for you / even when I'm down". By this point, having offered the song as an artistic endeavour, she has already "come up singing", making this final observation either unnecessary or a neat Möbius-strip twist that allows us to traverse seamlessly from inside to outside the narrative. The beginning of the song also offers such a device, with Ian offer-ing four introductory lines in a slightly different style to the rest of the song in which she claims she "was never one for singing / what I really feel", a strangely unconvincing assertion from the author of 'Society's Child' and 'At Seventeen', the enormously successful hit she would subsequently release in 1975.

Nina Simone included a rendition of 'Stars' in her set at the 1976 Mon-treux Jazz Festival. It is worth giving a brief overview of the performance leading up to this rendition both as a way of framing 'Stars' and as a snap-shot of this moment of lateness in Simone's career. Prior to her appearance at the festival, Simone had been living away from the USA for a number of years, first temporarily in Barbados, then for a longer period in Liberia. She had not appeared at Montreux since 1968 and was given an enthusiastic reception after being announced by festival organizer Claude Nobs. Simone must have unsettled many with her first gestures; following a long bow, she stood at the front of the stage staring out into the audience for more than

30 seconds, a long time in such a setting (and when viewing the recording of the concert), then sat down at the piano and began to compose herself (F3). In a voice alternating between soothing intimacy and a harder-edged tone, Simone announces her return but declares that she will not be doing any more jazz festivals after this one as she will "graduate to a higher class". She then announces that "We will start from the beginning" and plays the familiar "Wenceslas" theme that introduces 'Little Girl Blue'. The ensuing version is notable for a number of lyrical changes, most obviously the repeated references to "liberated little girl blue" and "little lady, Miss Sadie". Simone sings the line "all you can count on is yourself" as if she is reflecting on her own situation, a feeling that also comes when she adds the lines "ain't no use to try to tell them / they wouldn't understand if you tried to tell them". The close of the song involves Simone playing the "Wenceslas" theme, improvising new piano and vocal lines (including African terms) and appearing to finish the track by leaping from her piano stool, only to return to sing the closing lines once more.

In one of many lengthy spoken interludes, Simone tells her audience that they have not seen her for a while because she "went home", a reference to her two years in Liberia. She then offers an even more physical, keyboard-pummelling rendition of 'Backlash Blues' than that witnessed on the *Live in '65 & '68* video recording; ample evidence of Simone's ability to use the piano as a rhythm instrument is provided when she engages the drummer in a percussive duet. There follows an intense version of 'Be My Husband' in which Simone performs at the front of the stage accompanied only by the drums. Part way through she takes a break from singing and dancing to inform the audience, "I made 35 albums, they bootlegged 70. Everybody took a chunk of me". She then proceeds to tell them about watching "Janis Joplin's film" and about how Joplin's tragic story had affected her. In one of the highlights of an astonishing set, Simone proceeds to the version of 'I Wish I Knew How It Would Feel To Be Free' discussed earlier, punctuating the line "I wish you could know . . . what it means . . . to be me" with violent stabs at the piano keyboard that emphasize the line and further the sense that we are watching a more than usually naked, confessional performance.

Simone then leaves the stage, returning a few minutes later for an encore. It is at this point that she performs 'Stars', prefacing it with the observation "I'm tired. You don't know what I mean" and informing the audience that she hopes they will "see this spirit in another sphere" very soon. She describes

Janis Ian's song as "the only way to tell you who I am these days" and indicates that this is because of current critical and popular opinion of her, Simone: "'She used to be a star and she's gone all the way to the bottom'". She then embarks upon a series of barely connected points – including a call-out to David Bowie, who she believes is in the audience, and a reference to her necklace, which is "fit for a queen" – before suddenly launching into the refrain of 'Stars'. After barely two lines, Simone stops to order an audience member to sit down. Once satisfied that they have, she relaunches 'Stars', slowly and majestically rendering all the pathos of Ian's lyric with the use of dramatic pauses, whispers and the lightest of touches on the keyboard. As she stares intensely at the crowd and whispers the lyrics, it is easy to believe that this really is "who she is".

When Simone reaches the line in Ian's song about not owning one's name (which she slightly rephrases to "using a name you've never owned"), she stares into the audience as if to re-emphasize that she feels used by the record industry. She also personalizes the refrain, converting it from "they always have a story" to "I'm trying to tell my story" and adds, "Janis Ian told it very well. Janis Joplin told it even better. Billie Holiday told it even better". Subsequently, the line becomes "we always have a story", placing Simone among the pantheon of other stars she has already named. Simone uses an extemporization on the "we always have a story" to steer the tune towards a modulation, from which she switches abruptly to a version of Morris Albert's 'Feelings', which had been a hit the previous year. At one point she breaks off to exclaim, "I do not believe the conditions that produced a situation that demanded a song like that"; it is not clear whether she is referring to Albert's song or to Ian's. It is interesting that Simone chooses this song, having omitted the line about never "singing what I really feel" that prefaces Ian's version of 'Stars'. Miles away from that ironically distancing move, Simone's medley of 'Stars' and 'Feelings', like the rest of her edge-of-the-seat festival set, is about nothing if not singing what she feels.

From the start of 'Stars' to the closing note of 'Feelings' and Simone's shouted "Goodnight!" there are seventeen minutes in which she absolutely inhabits the two songs. The sense of involvement in a highly personal moment is palpable, and witnessing the recorded performance even (or especially) at this temporal and spatial remove is an exhausting yet intensely moving experience. Throughout her 1976 Montreux set, and particularly during 'Stars / Feelings', Simone's embodiment of age, experience and weary sincerity not only makes for a compelling performance, but also attests to a lateness that combines biography-as-confession with unresolved yearning. These are features that would become ever more prevalent in the chronologically late work she produced.

'My Father'

A number of the foregoing issues are further developed in Simone's version of Judy Collins's 'My Father', a song imbued with a strong autobiographical element for Simone. 'My Father' appeared on Collins's *Who Knows Where the Time Goes* and tells of the promises made by the narrator's father, the most memorable of which involves living in France and "boating on the Seine". The song operates as a kind of memoir, as the narrator recalls her childhood in Ohio, her father working in the mines and the dreams he would share with his daughters. A second verse adds mature experience, recording the disappearance of the narrator's sisters to the distant cities of Denver and Cheyenne. Left behind, she witnesses the disappearance, too, of her father's dreams, the colours of which "faded without a sound". The third verse moves to the present, where we find the narrator living in France with her children and telling tales of her father's life; perhaps her father is living with them, staying true to his promise, for the closing lines describe the narrator watching "the Paris sun / set in my father's eyes again" (C9, track 13).

Collins's father was a blind singer and radio broadcaster who, by her own accounts, had a strong influence on his daughter's life (J. Collins 2003). He died in 1967 and there is little doubt that this song was inspired by his passing. That said, it is not "autobiographical" in the sense of being *all* about Collins or her father. He is not the miner mentioned in the first and third verses, the family did not live in Ohio and Collins did not have any older sisters. As for the role of Paris in the song, this seems to be entirely fictional, though we cannot be sure of the veracity of the father's promise. Clearly, then, the song is a fictional narrative, written and sung by Collins as both author and vocal actor. Yet the sadness of the melody, the sense of loss evoked by the lyrics and the reference to the sun setting in her father's (blind?) eyes cannot help but evoke the notion of a direct remembrance of Collins's own late father.

Nina Simone, of course, approached the song as a cover version, a move we might assume would further remove the possibility of any authorial connection to a father that might be considered "hers". Yet, in much the same way that Collins's fictional song is still somehow *about* her and her father, so

Simone's reading removes the fiction dividing the song's singer from its subject. A fragment of a recording session released in 1998 shows that the singer intended to cut the song in 1971. This suggests that she had been listening to Collins's *Who Knows Where the Time Goes*, the title song of which she had recorded in late 1969. In this first recorded attempt, Simone changes the first line to "My father always promised me", but then only gets through six lines of the first verse, stopping after "He worked in the mines" to declare to those assembled in the studio, "I don't want to sing this song. It's not [for?] me. [Pause] My father always promised me that we would be free but he did not promise me that we would live in France." Simone then collapses into laughter. A male voice asks "How about Brooklyn?" to which Simone immediately responds, "No. My father knew nothing about New York at all. He promised me that we would live in peace. And that maybe I can still get." She then removes the song from consideration in that session (B19, disc 2, track 11).

Simone did come back to the song later, including a version on *Baltimore* (1978), her first album of new recordings for many years (B6, track 4). She was later dismissive of the album, claiming she had had no control over the choice of material, but this seems doubtful in the case of 'My Father' given the attempt to record the song earlier in the decade. Simone presents the song as three verses, omitting Collins's fourth verse. As in the earlier reading, she sings "My father always promised me", singularizing the object pronoun. Other notable changes include her adjustment of the last line of each verse. In the first, she hovers on the final word "time", letting it drift for six seconds (1:27 to 1:33) so that it becomes more of a hum or drone than a word, before resolving the melody with a repeat of the last two words, "in time". In the second verse a similar expectation is set up in the second half by a slight vocal drone on "alone". Simone then alters Collins's words to sing the couplet "Hoping that my father's dreams / would someday take me home". "Home" features a vocal drone (2:50 to 2:53), aligning it with the end of the previous verse ("time") and with "alone" from this verse. There is a slightly longer pause than in the previous verse and then a repetition of "take me home". At the close of the third and final verse, Simone again alters the lyrics, seemingly due to a mistake: "And watch my father's eyes watch the setting sun / Set in my father's eyes . . . again". At the place where the vocal drone had been in the earlier verses, she offers the word "eyes" (4:17 to 4:22), starting out on the same droning note as before but quickly moving into a soft melisma that lets the word float briefly before the resolution of "again". Simone's reading of the song, then, serves to emphasize crucial words to underline a narrative of loss and yearning. Meanwhile, this yearning is backed up by an aching string arrangement that builds gradually during the first verse and then soars at significant moments of the narrative in the second and third verses: "grown up dreams", "danced alone", "children dance and sing", "I sail my memories of home".

The words that Simone emphasizes – time, alone, home, eyes – may remind us of a relationship made by Walter Benjamin between gaze and familiarity: "Inherent in the gaze . . . is the expectation that it will be returned by that on which it is bestowed. Where this expectation is met (which, in the case of thought processes, can apply equally to an intentional gaze of awareness and to a glance pure and simple), there is an experience [*Erfahrung*] of the aura in all its fullness" (2006, 338). Benjamin uses this concept to suggest that Baudelaire's poetry is one that highlights the destruction of the aura – and hence embraces modernity – in its preoccupation with the unreturned gaze: "What happens here is that the expectation aroused by the gaze of the human eye is not fulfilled. Baudelaire describes eyes that could be said to have lost their ability to look" (339). As Eric Santner observes, Benjamin makes a distinction between an acceptance, initiated by Baudelaire, of modern experience (*Erlebnis*) and a nostalgia for premodern experience (*Erfahrung*), the latter associated with home and the familiar in all of its connotations. Paraphrasing Benjamin, Santner writes, "Home . . . is first and foremost that place . . . where one finds the aura constituted by eyes that return a gaze" (1990, 121). The narrator of 'My Father' seems to articulate the quest for such a place. Home is here a remembered past but one that is never stable in that it resides in a place of constant dreaming, of escape. It is mostly spoken from a place described by Benjamin as "an intentional gaze" – or from memory, which we could figure as a search for a past that looks back at the searcher – but the only explicit reference to eyes is that of the final line of the third verse. In Collins's version, it is tempting to read into this lyric a reference to her father's blindness, to eyes that "have lost their ability to look", yet Simone's handling of these lines is perhaps more fascinating. The curious (Freudian? Lacanian?) slippage that leads to "watch my father's eyes watch the setting sun / Set in my father's eyes . . . again" compels us to dwell on the notion of the gaze. The sense of confusion here – who is watching what? – emphasizes gaze as process over any obvious sense of someone looking or someone or something being looked at. If we *do* pick apart the meaning, however, we seem to be left with this: where the "correct" version had a narrator watching the sun reflected in her father's (possibly blind) eyes, this version emphasizes the father's own watching, with the narrator's watching now resigned to a secondary place, a watching of a watching. It is tempting to read this secondary watching as a kind of determination, such as that settled on by Simone after what she felt was her father's betrayal of her trust. Overhearing him lie to one of her brothers about the importance of his role in the family – a role reduced in reality due to ill health – Simone was shocked and found herself making a vow not to see him again, a promise she kept even as he lay dying. Hers was a refusal of familiarity and home, a refusal to go back to a place that would return her gaze. The secondary watching described in the last line of 'My Father' can be read as the passive awareness of a daughter waiting for her father to die: "I knew I was hurting Daddy and myself more," she wrote, "but there was nothing I could do: I was helpless because of the vow I had made, the vow I had to obey" (Simone and Cleary 2003, 125).

This hurt was one that would continue to grow in Simone in later years, leading to regret that she had not reconciled herself with her father. It is perhaps the replacement of that earlier refusal of the gaze with a subsequent longing for it that explains Simone's return to 'My Father'. This certainly seems to be the case in the film *La Légende*, where the song is played over footage of Simone visiting her father's grave in Tryon, her home town. The father represents the lure of the promised land ("freedom", "peace", "France") which he cannot deliver, leaving the daughter to seek it out herself ("maybe that I can still find") even as she fears utopia may be not be a place that lies ahead but one she has abandoned long ago, leading to what Santner calls a "utopian libido . . . a yearning for a space of specular mutuality". Furthermore, "The absence of a space where eyes return a gaze initiates . . . all those quests for and conquests of new territories of auratic experience, new searches for the gaze that would finally authenticate one's worth and reality" (1990, 122). In this context it is worth repeating Simone's view of this search: "Sometimes I think the whole of my life has been a search to find the one place I truly belong" (Simone and Cleary 2003, 113).

Simone's recorded output after *Baltimore* was sparse. She made an album in France in 1982 entitled *Fodder on My Wings* and bearing a dedication to "My father", but the album was little known outside her French fan base. It is noteworthy, with regard to Simone's late voice, for her harrowing version of Gilbert O'Sullivan's 'Alone Again Naturally', in which Simone completely dispenses with the original verses and replaces them with lyrics written about her father's final days. The determination that I read into her versions of 'My Father' is strongly emphasized here in lines such as "Now he's fading away / and I'm glad to say / He's dying at last, naturally". The first verse speaks of "Blinded eyes still searching / For some distant dream / that had faded away at the seams", providing another link with 'My Father' and allowing us to read back the unmentioned blindness of Collins's father into that song (B8, track 6; see also Simone and Cleary 2003, 126–8).

To Be Frank

Simone's next studio album, *Nina's Back*, was recorded in 1985 in New York, after which there were some live albums but no studio recording until her final album *A Single Woman* (1993). The final two studio albums both contain versions of songs associated with Frank Sinatra's late 1960s period. These songs all come from two albums recorded by Sinatra in 1969, *A Man Alone* and *Watertown*, both notable for being song suites created especially for Sinatra to perform and written with a particular image of Sinatra in mind. In the case of *A Man Alone*, Rod McKuen, a highly successful pop-poet and translator of Jacques Brel's songs, provided the kind of material suited to Sinatra's more vulnerable side. *Watertown*, written by Jake Holmes and Bob Gaudio, was an attempt to take Sinatra further into "abandoned male" territory than he had previously been and was a concept album that told the story of a father attempting to bring up his two children and get over his loss after his wife leaves their small Midwestern town for a new life in the big city.

Although not Sinatra's best known or critically lauded work, Nina Simone clearly heard something in these albums. The first recording she made of the material was a version of 'For a While', a track from *Watertown* (C36, track 3; B14, track 4). The song's lyricist Jake Holmes said of the song:

> I've always felt that there is that moment in your life, when you forget about something that is really terrible. For five minutes the sun is shining and everything is beautiful. Then all of a sudden you realize that the person you cared about is gone, and it all comes back. It is one of those horrible things about grief – one of those little holes in grief when it becomes even more painful (C36, liner notes).

The memory process Holmes describes resembles the Proustian "rush" that interrupts the everyday with the shock of all that has been lost. The song opens with the line "Lost in day to day", suggesting that radical, unassimilated loss has been covered over – made distant – by a more homely loss associated with the mundane. The narrator gets by *comme d'habitude* and "days go by with no empty feeling", until, that is, the Proustian moments when "I remember you're gone". The sentiment here is remarkably similar to an earlier song that Sinatra and Simone (and Billie Holiday) had recorded, Hoagy Carmichael's 'I Get Along Without You Very Well', with its famous list of exceptions: "except when soft rains fall", "except when I hear your name", "except perhaps in Spring". A notable difference resides in the fact that Carmichael's protagonist recognizes that (s)he should not let these moments happen: "But then I should never ever think of Spring / For that would surely break my heart in two". Holmes has his protagonist rebuke his friends for trying to keep, or find, him company: "They forget that I'm not over you / For a while". He has twisted the title's meaning to suggest that he wants to hang on to this longing; rather than mourn and move on, he wishes to remain melancholy.

For Simone, drifting increasingly between mourning and melancholy, it was an ideal song to perform. The version she recorded for *Nina's Back* is not notable musically, in that she is backed by a group whose mid-1980s jazz-rock – overemphasized by the production – provides an arrangement that threatens to overwhelm the lyric. However, what Simone does with the lyric *is* notable, especially for any listener who has more than a passing interest in the artist's career and personal life (arguably a large proportion of those still buying new Simone recordings in 1985). She delivers the first verse unchanged, but changes a line in the second from "some work I've got to do" to "some music I've got to do". The alteration is small but telling and sets us up for the next changes: firstly the addition of the phrase "I touch my hair and I touch my skin" just before "I remember you're gone"; secondly, the lines "People say to me / Nina, you need some company". If we had been unsure before, there now seems little doubt that this is a song about Simone herself. Where the gap between the vocal actor and the "I" of Sinatra's version had been emphasized due to the song's inclusion in a concept album told from the point of view of an obviously fictional narrator (albeit voiced by a singer whose vocal act was crucial to the believability of the work), here the song is removed from its context and personalized in a way that suggests two things about the singer. Firstly, she is describing her desire to sublimate the loss she feels with "some music I've got to do": on the one hand, *"doing" the music will stop me from drifting into melancholy*; on the other, *I have to do it, it is what keeps me going* (the song immediately preceding 'For a While' is Simone's own composition, 'I Sing Just to Know that I'm Alive'). Secondly, she is recognizing that the losses of her life are ones she is far from being "over". Who or what is "you" in this case? Her autobiography would soon provide some possible answers: her father, the various men in her life from her childhood sweetheart Edney onwards, the civil rights movement, the denial of her childhood ambitions to be a concert pianist. During a 1984 performance at Ronnie Scott's in London, Simone dedicated the song to "my lover who is gone from me, from Liberia, West Africa" and added a coda borrowed from her song 'If You Knew' addressed to "CC" (F4). As her autobiography reveals, both these references are to C. C. Dennis, her "Liberian Rhett Butler" (Simone and Cleary 2003, 143–50). Dennis abandoned his plans to marry her and left her for another woman. This does not necessarily solve the dilemma as to who the "you" of 'For a While' might be; as Simone writes, "my reaction to losing C.C. was similar to the way I felt after Daddy died" (149). The 1984 dedication is no doubt a reference to Dennis's death shortly after the 1980 coup in Liberia as much as it is to his leaving her; like her father, he had left her twice, once in life and once in death. In memory, as Freud pointed out, such events are likely to be conflated into a single moment (1962, 299–322). The "screen memory" Simone articulates with 'For a While' no doubt conflates many such episodes, as indeed it does for us as listeners projecting the song onto our own acoustic screens. Perhaps the "you" is Nina Simone herself: "I touch my hair and I touch my skin" anticipates the passage in her autobiography where she undergoes the late 1960s "mirror stage" described at the beginning of this chapter. The realization of who she was and who she could have been led to a mourning of her own potential. We can read the documents of the early 1990s – *I Put a Spell on You*, *La Légende* and *A Single Woman* – as attempts to find, via the mediation of memory in print, film and disc, a promise lost in time.

In 1993 Simone appropriated more Sinatra material, this time three songs from *A Man Alone*. An interview with Michael Alago, the executive responsible for signing Simone to Elektra, provides a fascinating conflation of two figures who loomed large in Simone's life and career:

> Nina and I fashioned the album so that it was like a hom-
> age to the Frank Sinatra album *A Man Alone*. Nina loved that
> album and we both adored Rod McKuen. It turned out to be
> a beautiful recording of love, loneliness and loss, as a homage
> to both Frank and her late father (quoted in Hampton and
> Nathan 2004, 169).

The album opens with 'A Single Woman', Simone's version of 'The Single Man' from the Sinatra/McKuen album (C35, track 1; B17, track 1). From the outset it paints a portrait of loneliness as we hear the familiar voice, now deepened with age, sing "I live alone / That hasn't always been / Easy to do". She hears voices in the walls of her house that tell her yesterday was "a better day". The song places us in a home that the third verse tells us "once . . . was filled / with love", albeit that the narrator "can't remember when". Whereas in 'My Father', she had both sought and defied the eyes that might return a gaze, here she seems to be in thrall to (imprisoned by) walls that return a voice. They are familiar, comfortable and plastered in melancholy. Outside these walls, as we hear in the second verse, the loneliness is equally acute: she is alone even in a crowd and "caught in a world / Few people understand". Simone seems to be talking about her own world (of faded glory, occasional fame and depression) rather than the world of modernity ushered in by the unreturned gazes of the crowd in Baudelaire's and Benjamin's cityscapes. Perhaps, as suggested in Chapter 1, Simone is a symptom of that very history, attached as it is to a particular dehumanizing cultural trauma of which she could be said to be a product. But at this stage of her career, at this stage of the fantasy of authentication, such thoughts seem far away, tethered to a realm of constructivist knowledge that could not allow Simone the singularity she claims here.

Simone uses this singularity to add conviction to the other songs she covers from *A Man Alone*. The first of these is 'Lonesome Cities', a tale that mixes experience with wanderlust to paint a picture of a (sexual and geographical) explorer who is not yet ready to stop but who realizes that she won't be able to "run away from me". The second is 'Love's Been Good to Me', another song of experience about a roamer who has "never found a home" but is comforted by the memories of past loves. The changes to the songs are unsurprising and relate mostly to gendered pronouns.

As we saw at the beginning of this book, with the concept of the traumatic event we have moved away from Alain Badiou's theorization of event while retaining some of his vocabulary. Badiou's question is how something new emerges, hence the aptness of his work in thinking about revolutionary moments. In his example of love the emphasis is very much on the emergence of an amorous relationship and the fidelity shown to it. He does not, however, have much to say about the end of the relationship – this is where thinking about the traumatic event comes in. When love breaks down (or rather when a relationship breaks down, for love itself has a tendency to persevere) there can be a change as relevant to the person's future as when it starts. We can also identify moments that exceed the situation of the break-up, making it an event in Badiouian terms; here, psychoanalysis may be more useful in that, rather than being preoccupied with the emergence of the new, it is more interested in the past, in dealing with the ways the new (in the form of the symptom) plays havoc with the subject. One should not pledge fidelity to one's symptom but rather, as Lacan and Badiou both remind us, to one's desire. And if love is the area which shows this split the most effectively, it is worth dwelling on Nina Simone's love songs as much as on her revolutionary material. Ntozake Shange makes a similar point in her comments on Simone's final album, suggesting that its preoccupation with romance is as relevant as Simone's earlier commitment to the movement:

> A *Single Woman* is about love, all kinds of love. Especially, a full grown woman in love. A woman in the process of defining her life, deciding her fate, accepting, without shame or guilt, her own needs and desires. With a voice, that unmistakable Simone voice, worldly, yet vulnerable, this album allows us the experiences only a strong woman survives . . . Depending on how well we've been loved or not loved, these lyrics and the earned authority of Simone's voice will bring hope, reassurance, or the right to grieve (B17, liner notes).

What is notable here is the similarity to observations that have been made in relation to the "worldly, yet vulnerable" Frank Sinatra. Perhaps it is worth noting, in addition to Shange's points, that Simone here has somehow managed to wrest the mantle of the male master. But perhaps Simone is not ultimately claiming something that the male (i.e. Sinatra) was always in possession of. Perhaps she is reclaiming a subject position stolen from the feminine, re-igniting torch singing as *écriture feminine*, a refusal of – and, paradoxically, a simultaneous dependence on – the law as perfected in torch singing. There needs, after all, to be a space for the enunciation of failure. However much she and we might want it to be otherwise, Simone's is not ultimately a victory song.

Conclusion

Simone's song may not have been one of victory but she produced many victorious moments, moments in which her artistry communicated unambiguous meaning to her audience. One of the most unambiguous messages it sent was that if we were always in danger of being too late to the show, if we were always going "too slow", if we did not speed up and change our ways of thinking, living and loving, we could only expect a deserved apocalypse. Whether that fate was to "die like flies" or to suffer the limbo of unquenched desires and unrealized visions, Simone's music told of a time to come. In bringing together the time to come of the torch singer's desperate hope (a hope born of unrequited love) or the protest singer's vision of Messianic change, Simone adopted a late voice that included the kind of biographical aspects discussed in this chapter while also surpassing the biographical to take a reading of the "end times" in which she was living.

This late voice can be said to be a voice subject to chronology, but also a sound produced by a vocal actor. It is a voice that navigates the twisted routes of innocence and experience, that knows that the time goes but may not know where it goes. It is a voice that looks back and that admits defeat, having recognized that "a dream deferred" will "dry up / like a raisin in the sun / Or fester like a sore" (Hughes 1995, 426). But the late voice is still, in Simone's case, an angry voice, one that will not go gently, which does not flinch but may sometimes sag from the weight of bearing witness. It is a voice that speaks of a wound which refuses to heal, that follows bearing witness with a baring of the soul, that imagines a different history, another spring, that presents a future anteriority, a voice that comes from after now, from an "archaeology of the future" (Jameson 2005), a voice that visits the present to "abduct" its listeners to the promise of the future (Eshun 1998). It is, finally, a voice still able to put a spell on its listeners.

5 Legacy

Nina Simone's late voice was not only one of longing and return; it remained an angry one. Although she continued to perform sporadically up until the late 1990s, she was known as a difficult performer, an often obstreperous diva-figure. A book published after her death by long-term friend Sylvia Hampton describes a woman driven by demons due to "the devastating effects of a mental disorder that left her incapable of maintaining the emotional constancy she craved" (Hampton and Nathan 2004, 9). Hampton spares few details in her descriptions of Simone's occasional cruelty to her and her brother. One of the reasons for Simone's ire seems to be her dwindling celebrity following her self-imposed exile and reclusion. It is this increasing invisibility (and inaudibility) that most other commentators on Simone emphasize, even as they highlight her importance to the 1960s. Comparing Simone to other black artists who successfully connected with the times, Philip Ennis writes,

> Nina Simone was not as fortunate. Her decision to leave the States in late 1969 symbolized the impasse of black pop. She earned the name "the High Priestess of Soul" the hard way, taking the condition of her people seriously enough to reject the ordinary settings in which black artists could speak and sing. She went beyond the boundaries of commercial R&B, could not enter gospel, was not invited into jazz very warmly, and, of course, never came anywhere near rock. She neither chose nor could find an organized political platform from which to concertize her ideas. Simone drove herself musically out of mainstream black cultural and political circles and ended up in a burning rage that took her out of America and into the shelter of Europe. Like almost all those who fought too far out past their audiences' musical tastes and political understanding, she fell harder than those who went easier. Some of rock's warriors would sadly soon follow this path (1992, 348).

In this account it was Simone's eclecticism that led to her downfall. It is interesting to note the connection made by Ennis between Simone's misfortune and that of the "warriors", often figured as the exemplary figures of loss in rock mythology and elsewhere, suggesting that the loss of rock's romantic moment is more pertinent to many popular culture historians than the unrealized dreams of black music in the 1960s. Lucy O'Brien, describing an interview with Simone in 1992, focuses instead on Simone's own unrealized dreams:

> Her life story is packed with "should have beens". She should have become America's first black classical pianist, but the only realistic route open for a poor unknown black girl in the 1950s was supper-club swing or a strong dose of the blues. She should have been happily married with 2.2 kids and a white picket fence. Instead the rigours of the road left her with two failed marriages and a string of abandoned lovers (2002, 59).

In an obituary in *The Wire*, Ian Penman recalled the incident from Simone's childhood when, following an attempt by a white family to move Simone's parents from the front row of her first public piano recital and the child's demand that they stay there, the audience laughed at her assertive ways. Penman's Simone is a singer haunted by traumatic memories: "It becomes easier to understand her 'tantrums' or the difficulty she often found with performing if you remember that every stage was perhaps haunted by the spectres of that first recital". Penman takes the issue of haunting further:

> To these ears, the use of the word "diva" to pigeonhole her later in her career was just one more attempt – no matter how well intentioned – to pretend her skin wasn't there, made no difference, fell away somehow the moment she took to a stage. To pretend there was no pain, no politics; to jeer and laugh one more time at . . . funny Nina, wonky Nina, obstreperous Nina, Nina with the outsize dreams . . . (2003, 26).

Indeed, the word "diva" does a lot of contradictory work. Although Simone had been quick to apply the term to herself from at least the late 1960s – part of her self-alignment with Maria Callas and no doubt also a pointed reminder to her interlocutors of her abilities as a classical artist – the application of the word by others could be read in different ways. As Michel Poizat points out, the term, as it became attached to the opera star, had important connections to power:

> What is new in the appellation "diva" is that now it is the female singer and she alone who is accorded divine status, as though it were her power to transform herself into pure voice, inasmuch as she is *one* incarnation of *many* successive roles, that allowed her to be divine (1992, 180, original emphasis).

The "successive roles" articulated by a single performer could connect with my earlier discussion of Simone as a vocal actor, while the focus on the "divine" may remind us of the appellation "High Priestess" applied to the singer. Yet, more in line with Penman's reading of the word, Poizat goes on to say:

> The term "diva" admits of another, incidental connotation in its application to the great female vocal artists, a connotation of what I have referred to as "the mad law," the caprice. Behind the title "diva" there is often the somewhat pejorative idea of capricious behavior, bizarre demands, in short, the abuse of a position of absolute mastery (1992, 180).

Again, it is worth remembering that "capricious" is a word that Simone was seemingly content to use about herself (see, for example, her interviews in *La Légende*). Of course, she may well have learned to use such terms to deflect further intrusion into her psychic world, but there can be no denying the pleasure with which she seems to speak of her capricious and occasionally cruel side. In this sense, the word "diva" combines divine power with cruelty.

Remembering Simone

While Simone's work had been neglected to a certain extent up until her death, she was never completely forgotten. This was especially the case in popular culture, where the singer was mentioned in numerous popular songs, films and magazines. At the time of her revolutionary height, The Last Poets named her in their song "Black Wish" (on the 1970 album *The Last Poets* [C26, disc 1, track 10]), claiming "I am the wish that makes Nina Simone wish she knew how it felt to be free", a reference to Simone's famous song. A generation later, Lauryn Hill of The Fugees could be found boasting on 'Ready or Not', "While you imitatin' Al Capone / I be Nina Simone and defecatin' on your microphone", which, according to Mark Anthony Neal (2003), represented "an effort to distinguish [Hill's] womanist musings from the gangsterization of mainstream hip-hop". Meanwhile, Joe Strummer and the Mescaleros gave a shout out to the singer on the track of *Global A Go-Go* album (2001): 'Nina Simone over Sierra Leone'.

Simone was a frequently audible presence in the 1993 film *Point of No Return* (also known as *The Assassin*), where the protagonist, played by Bridget Fonda, is a "reformed" drug addict turned government killer who is obsessed by Simone's music and takes the codename "Nina". At one point in the film Simone's voice is fitted to a gaze "Nina" casts at the sea outside her apartment shortly after she has been released from the training facility where she had been held; as we partake of her sense of freedom, the opening lines of 'Feeling Good' anchor the emotion: "Birds flyin' high, you know how I feel / Sun in the sky, you know how I feel". At another point it becomes clear that Simone's voice is associated with the heroine's mother. After her boyfriend asks why she always plays Simone's music when she is upset, she says that it was the music she grew up listening to: "It sounded so passionate, so savage, all about love and loss". Following her death, Simone was remembered in the closing section of Richard Linklater's *Before Sunset* (2004), a film preoccupied with loss, unrealized ambition, enslavement to the past and memories. As the two protagonists mourn Simone's passing, a recording of her singing 'Just in Time' serves to summarize the topics of the film and sets up the viewer's reflections as it moves from the final scene into the credits. Simone also features in the end credits to the film adaptation of Ntozake Shange's *For Colored Girls* (2010), where a four-voiced version of 'Four Women' is constructed from a sample of Simone's original recording, followed by newly recorded verses by Simone's daughter Lisa, Laura Izibor and Ledizi. The recording realizes the multi-vocal possibility always suggested by the song while also partly telling the story of the "suicidal" women depicted in Shange's drama and connecting Simone to a new sisterhood.

Simone's own songs and her interpretations of other songs led to a number of cover versions, or versions based on her interpretations, from quite early in her career. The Animals were influenced by her version of 'Don't Let Me Be Misunderstood', which they recorded in 1965, while former Animal Alan Price recorded 'I Put a Spell On You', a song that Simone had given a distinctive reading. Simone's most covered song was one co-written by her and her bandleader Weldon Irvine. 'To Be Young, Gifted and Black' was a tribute to Simone's friend (and one of the main reasons for her involvement in the civil rights movement), the playwright Lorraine Hansberry. The song was famously recorded by Aretha Franklin, whose reading, in Peter Guralnick's words, was "a joyous celebration of negritude" (1986, 349); other notable versions were made popular by Donny Hathaway, Dionne Warwick and Bob & Marcia, the latter providing the template for numerous reggae versions throughout the 1970s. More recent covers have included: Jeff Buckley's reading of 'Lilac Wine' (on *Grace*, 1996), which he based on Simone's 1965 version, and his 'Be Your Husband', an adaptation of Simone's 'Be My Husband'; rock band Muse's version of 'Feeling Good' on their *Origin of Symmetry* album (2001), the song also becoming a feature of their live concerts; Americana band The Walkabouts' EP *Slow Days With Nina* (2005), featuring a handful of songs associated with Simone; and flamenco singer Estrella Morente's inclusion of 'Ne Me Quitte Pas' as a homage to Simone on her womanist album *Mujeres* (2006). 2006 also saw the release of *Nina Simone Remixed & Reimagined*, which highlighted a trend towards raiding the singer's back catalogue for mixable material. Other mixes were featured on the *Verve Remixed* album, while at least one white label twelve-inch single of Simone remixes circulated amongst DJs in the mid-2000s.

Simone has also been a notable influence on other musicians, even when there have not been explicit references. As mentioned earlier in this book, one example is Roberta Flack, whose repertoire overlapped with, and whose ambition was comparable to, Simone's. Flack performed a mixture of jazz, soul, folk, dramatic and piano-led reflective material that often, especially in tracks such as 'Our Ages or Our Hearts' (from *First Take*), with its repeated lines and interjections, expressed a similar vocal delivery to Simone. Flack, along with other singers of her generation who were either already in, or would move towards, soul music in the 1970s, represented a continuing voice of conscience that took on the burden that Simone's voice had carried. In a posthumous tribute to Simone, Mark Anthony Neal somewhat revises the centrality he had placed on Marvin Gaye's *What's Going On* in his earlier (1999) work and shifts the focus of influence to Simone:

> Literally all of the mainstream protest music recorded by Black artists in the late 1960s and early 1970s, like Sly and the Family Stone's 'Thank You (Falletinme Be Mice Elf Agin)', The Temptations' 'Ball of Confusion', Freda Payne's 'Bring the Boys Home', Roberta Flack's 'Compared to What?,' Marvin Gaye's *What's Going On*, and Stevie Wonder's *Innervisions*, were indebted to 'Mississippi Goddam' (2003).

Neal pays tribute not only to Simone's art but to her importance as a historical reference point for a number of later musicians. As others have also pointed out, Simone was an influence on a number of new soul figures of more recent years such as Erykah Badu, Mary J. Blige (who, at the time of writing, had been cast to play Simone in a biopic of the artist) and Lauryn Hill, whose group The Fugees, as well as name-checking Simone, had a massive hit in 1996 with their version of Roberta Flack's 'Killing Me Softly With His Song'.

One interesting development since Simone's death has been the gradual (re)acceptance of her music as jazz. This may seem like a strange assertion, given that Simone is regularly filed in jazz sections of record stores and was marketed at the outset and the culmination of her career as a jazz artist. However, anyone researching the artist's life and work will be struck by the absence of references to her in popular and scholarly books about jazz. As has been suggested numerous times in this book, Simone's eclecticism ultimately barred her from inclusion in most accounts of music that defined themselves according to genre or style. This seems to have changed somewhat in recent years. One reason for this may be, as Will Friedwald suggests, a recognition that many jazz singers whose careers took off in the 1990s and 2000s sought a more eclectic range of sources to draw from and therefore saw Simone as an obvious influence (Friedwald 2010). This is arguably the case with Cassandra Wilson, who recalls Simone as much through her eclecticism as through her musical style.

There have been specifically jazz-oriented tributes to Simone, including entire albums by Barb Jungr and Kellylee Evans. These projects raise interesting questions about what happens when Simone is treated as an author and a jazz artist, at least a particular kind of jazz artist. Jungr's album, entitled *Just Like A Woman (Hymn to Nina)*, contains no songs written by Simone, but instead is a collection of "songs previously recorded by Nina Simone" and "dedicated to her" (C23). While it has been argued consistently throughout this book that Simone was able to take possession of other writers' material in a manner that could be heard as "authorial", "authoritative" and "authentic" (and clearly these words are connected by more than etymology), the act of presenting such songs as Simone's when the performances are Jungr's must inevitably reduce these factors. It has already been suggested that other artists' versions of songs that Simone covered still bear a connection to her and that should be even more the case when we experience a whole album of songs connected to Simone, even if we hear them at a remove. However, the deliberation of collecting the songs together under the title "Hymn to Nina" also forces us to think about Simone's entire oeuvre and to wonder at the exclusion of her self-written material, especially her protest material. Although two of the three Bob Dylan songs included stem from Dylan's "protest period" ('The Times They Are A-Changin'' and 'The Ballad of Hollis Brown'), the titling of the album after Dylan's 'Just Like A Woman' serves to recall Judy Collins's Dylan tribute album of the same name and Jungr's own Dylan tribute *Every Grain of Sand*, such are the intertextual levels at play in the circulation of cover versions.

The Nina Simone of Jungr's collection emerges as a performer of mainly romantic songs, an impression also given by Kellylee Evans's album *Nina* (C12). Evans treats the material with due reverence and her performances help to recuperate Simone back into the jazz world, not only through the musical style employed, but also by accompanying press materials that affirm Simone as "one of jazz's greatest vocalists and pianists" (artist's website). There is much to admire about Evans's cool delivery of songs associated with Simone and she and her musicians bring a sensitivity of interpretation that recalls contemporary performers such as Cassandra Wilson. However, it is notable that, once again, there are no Simone originals and an absence of any of the explicitly political material that the artist was known for. Evans was reportedly invited by the French Plus Loin label to record an album of standards, which she then combined with a desire to record a Simone tribute album. For this reason, the exclusion of Simone originals is understandable, though we might still wonder why there is no 'Strange Fruit' (surely a standard by now, albeit an uncomfortable one), nor anything from the more explicitly Afro-centric part of Simone's repertoire.

Simone's daughter Lisa, operating under the confusing pseudonym "Simone", released a tribute to her mother in 2008 (C33). Again, it positions the repertoire in a jazz setting through the use of big band arrangements. These arrangements in themselves distinguish *Simone on Simone* from the quieter chamber jazz of Jungr and Evans and the difference is increased by the addition of a gospel edge on a number of the songs. In a liner note, Lisa describes starting her musical career, like her mother, in the church and this background comes through, in particular, on versions of 'Go to Hell', 'Feeling Good' and 'I Wish I Knew How It Would Feel To Be Free', the latter song given the choral response suggested in Nina's versions. Elsewhere, Lisa displays her background in Broadway shows with showy tunes like 'Work Song', 'Gal from Joe's' and 'I Hold No Grudge'. Lisa's voice, although generally quite different to her mother's (higher, purer, cleaner, thinner, more trained) occasionally seems to channel Nina. These vocal moments are arguably more effective tributes than the two most explicit references to the women's relationship, 'Music for Lovers' and 'Child in Me'. The former is a song by Bart Howard (writer of 'Fly Me to the Moon') and was recorded for (but not released on) *Nina Simone and Piano!*, Nina returning to it for the *Baltimore* album. It is the opening song of *Simone on Simone* and features as a collaboration between mother and daughter (Nina on piano, Lisa on vocals) recorded live in Ireland in the late 1990s. Nina, whose voice is the first heard on the album, thus gets to posthumously introduce her daughter's tribute to her, a peculiarity of lateness that phonography allows. Following this uncanny beginning, the song delivers the kind of grandstanding, melismatic vocal that had become the norm for soul divas over the previous two decades (as essayed by Whitney Houston, Celine Dion and Mariah Carey); the vocal work is impressive but seems to remove the song from Nina's sphere. Sentiment is not necessarily the problem – Nina was often sentimental – but perhaps a particular *kind* of sentiment that we are not used to hearing attached to the Simone name. It is also a quite different type of sentiment – and vocal style – than that used by Lisa for the rest of the album, with the exception of 'Child in Me', which opens intriguingly with the piano chords from 'Four Women' but then leads into a slightly mawkish tale of the daughter's experience of the mother.

For Women

I would like to focus in slightly more detail on the memory work done in hip hop in order to connect it to some of the themes I have been discussing and to Nina Simone. I do not mean to focus on Simone's views on hip hop but to highlight the way that the music has attempted to supplement its often-analysed concerns with the present (either as celebration of community or critique of society) with a branch of nostalgic or elegiac hip hop that has kept an eye focused on the past. The past has been an important aspect of the music almost from its inception, be it in the archaeological work involved in sourcing samples and celebrating the black cultural past or in the quickly formed notion of an "old skool" that new pretenders were to be referred back to for lessons in authenticity. As with so many of its other concerns, hip hop has its own language for this process, locating its screen memories in a place known as "back in the day" and providing, in the figure of the "homie" or "homeboy", a simultaneous embodiment of community and masculinist representation of the homeland that all nostalgia makes reference to. Here, I will focus on the work of rapper Talib Kweli, whose album *Reflection Eternal* (2000) was a critically lauded piece of memory work.

In rap music it is rare to find cover versions of previous rap tracks and yet the core process of constructing the backing to new tracks developed from a different type of (re)covering via the practice of sampling. As old recordings were cut up, scratched, sampled and reused to form new musical pieces, so dialogues were set up between artists and eras. Though samples were traditionally taken from old soul and rock performances it also became common to quote from other rap records, as when Jay-Z samples lines from Nas and Outkast on his track 'Rap Game / Crack Game'. Tricia Rose suggests that sampling "affirms black musical history and locates these 'past' sounds in the 'present'" (1994, 89). She believes such an affirmation needs to be made because of the short shelf-life black musical products have historically experienced relative to predominantly white genres such as rock. It could be argued that this has more to do with the total predominance of rock music over all genres. Yet Rose does have a valid point about the need (even duty) to research the less-heard musics of the past and that rap artists have a most effective way of going about this:

> For the most part, sampling, not unlike versioning practices
> in Caribbean musics, is about paying homage, an invocation

of another's voice to help you to say what you want to say. It is also a means of archival research, a process of musical and cultural archaeology (1994, 79).

The dialogue this allows between different eras becomes part of the very fabric of rap's sonic matrix, allowing for new meanings to be developed in new contexts. The sampled voice becomes an instrument interwoven with the rapper's vocal and adds texture to what is often already a multi-vocal performance. Rap music tends to work in verse form with the verse either separated by a chorus or punctuated with a repeated refrain. Talib Kweli and Hi-Tek use the "bringing back sweet memories" line from Ann Peebles's 'I Can't Stand the Rain' to set up an appropriate refrain between the reminiscences of 'Memories Live' (C25, track 7). A technique such as this should draw attention to the artifice at work in the multi-layered rap song but in fact it allows a continuation of the illusion that the rapper is addressing the listener as he/she talks over and around the alien chorus.

The alienating qualities of sampling will be considered below when discussing the use of Nina Simone's voice and music in remixes of her work. Before that, it is worth considering the connections between Kweli and Simone, artists who share a preoccupation with the conflation of personal and collective memory to their respective places in the black public sphere. More specific links between the two, however, can be found in the figure of Weldon Irvine and in Kweli's version of one of Simone's signature songs.

Weldon Irvine was one of the main musical collaborators of Nina Simone's career, working as organist and arranger on a number of her performances and albums. Simone approached Irvine to write the lyrics to 'To Be Young, Gifted and Black', a song which became well known not only through her version but through the versions mentioned above. In addition to his work with Simone, Irvine developed a solo career as a bandleader in the 1970s, releasing a number of acclaimed albums and paving the way for what would come to be known as "acid jazz". He also composed a number of musicals and continued to write songs for other performers, amassing some 500 compositions. In the 1990s he turned his attention to hip hop and became involved with MCs Mos Def and Talib Kweli. Irvine provided keyboard and string arrangements for Mos Def's *Black On Both Sides* (1999) and played keyboards on Kweli's 'Africa Dream' (on *Reflection Eternal*). Kweli, Mos Def and Q-Tip appeared on Irvine's *The Amadou Project: The Price of Freedom* (2000).

The second specific connection between Kweli and Simone is his inclusion of her song 'Four Women' on *Reflection Eternal*. Kweli entitles his version of the song 'For Women' and it is included as an extra track on the album. Kweli appears to have based his track not on the version of 'Four Women' that appears on *Wild Is the Wind*, but on a later live recording included on the *Live at Berkeley* album and on subsequent compilations (B11, track 10; C25, track 20). What is notable here, especially given the non-biographical reading of 'Four Women' offered in Chapter 2, is that Kweli has chosen, deliberately or not, to re-enact a version of the song in which Simone explicitly connected herself to her material. A story Simone tells about her mother during her introduction to the song also becomes Kweli's introduction as he stresses that the first, and presumably oldest, woman mentioned in the song, Aunt Sara, is still alive. Simone's point had been to highlight the fact that the song is not (only) a chronological account of black women's consciousness from emancipation to the militant 1960s but rather a narration of coexisting modes of black female consciousness and complex notions of identity. In the same way that Simone, as diva, voiced all these women, so, she seemed to suggest, are her black female listeners all these women. With the live recording, listening as witnessing conflates with listening as burden: all her auditors must bear witness to these roles and carry the weight.

Kweli uses Aunt Sara's longevity to suggest, as elsewhere on *Reflection Eternal*, the importance of paying attention to experience: as he says in his spoken preamble, "we can't forget our elders". Kweli may be referring to Simone at this point, but his point is taken up again in the verse relating to his meeting with Aunt Sara: "Just her presence was a blessing and her essence was a lesson . . . Livin' a century, the strength of her memories". Where Simone had mentioned in her spoken interlude that "Aunt Sara has lived long enough to see the full circle come round", Kweli extends the point to make the cyclical processes of identification (self and other) explicit: "She lived from nigger to coloured to negro to black / To Afro then African-American and right back to nigger". Where Aunt Sara had been a continuing identity for Simone (possibly based on her own mother and, by extension, to those aspects of her mother she found in herself), for Kweli, highlighting as he does the necessity to learn from previous generations, Sara represents a history lesson. This is certainly how Michael Eric Dyson reads Kweli's version:

> The entire song is a study in the narrative reconstruction of the fragmented elements of black survival and a cautionary tale against the racial amnesia that destroys the fabric of black collective memory. By appealing to Simone's rhetorical precedent, Kweli situates the song's heuristic logic inside the matrix of racial identity and cultural continuity. By baptizing Simone's sentiments in a hip-hop rhetorical form, Kweli raises new questions about the relation between history and contemporary social practice and fuses the generational ambitions of two gifted artists – himself and Simone – while depicting the distinct political imperatives that drive his art (2003, 300).

Dyson, like Mark Anthony Neal, is keen to locate a sense of history in black music that removes it from accusations of "presentism" and its accompanying association with commercialism and locates it rather in the ongoing formation of a "black public sphere". Other commentators, such as Ellis Cashmore, wish to do away with what Cashmore sees as the myth "of an unbroken continuum that stretches back from rap music through soul, gospel and negro spirituals to the African-derived slave traditions". Such a narrative does no justice to black culture's "intricacies or indeed hiatuses" (1997, 2). While needing to bear this in mind alongside Robin Kelley's not entirely dissimilar points discussed earlier, it still remains important to recognize in the work of Talib Kweli and fellow travellers the effective use of such a narrative in order to pursue cultural memory work.

One way to approach this might be to follow the suggestions made by Paul Gilroy in his discussion of two strands of black aesthetics. Recognizing the "breaks and interruptions" that destabilize any understanding of black cultural practices as "the unproblematic transmission of a fixed essence through time", Gilroy observes that "the invocation of tradition may itself be a distinct, though covert, response to the destabilizing flux of the postcontemporary world" (1993, 101). Acceptance of Gilroy's "breaks and interruptions" and Cashmore's "hiatuses" may help us to see how the "invocation of tradition" is articulated in music. It is also worth recalling the work of bell hooks, another thinker interested in the relationships between essentialism, anti-essentialism and strategies of memory. In the collection of essays to which she has given the title *Yearning*, hooks expresses, "with no shame", a surprising nostalgia for a childhood of segregated schools and communities

(1990, 34). This nostalgia – really a yearning for non-fragmented community – is reminiscent of that found in post-1989 Eastern European culture. Of interest here is hooks's enactment of what Svetlana Boym (2001) would see as a "critical nostalgia" – evidenced by hooks's re-employment of "humanizing survival strategies of the past" (hooks 1990, 39). Indeed, hooks highlights the active nature of memory herself: "Memory need not be a passive reflection, a nostalgic longing for things to be as they once were; it can function as a way of knowing and learning from the past . . . It can serve as a catalyst for self-recovery" (40). And, in keeping with the religious tone of such languages of faith, she concludes, "We need to sing again the old songs, those spirituals that renewed the spirits and made the journey sweet, hear again the old testimony urging us to keep the faith, to go forward in love" (40).

A Recorded Life

In many ways, we have circled back to the beginning of our narrative and the fact that Simone's legacy is a recorded one. A few questions still attach themselves to Simone's legacy, not least the value we place on those recordings. Roy Kasten poses one of these questions quite starkly in a memorial essay, asking "What has Nina Simone left us?" She "recorded too often, too quickly" in the 1960s, not allowing the space we require to distinguish her works from each other (2004, 145–6). As well as the ubiquity of her work in that period, there is also the fact that it appeared a long time ago and has not always remained available in its original form. While many artists from the period are remembered for the classics of that time, the fact that they are in some way still visible reminds us of them, whereas Simone, from the time she set off around the Black Atlantic, was out of sight and out of mind: "she sang until her body gave out [but] in her exile, few heard" (148). Robin Kelley also highlights how Simone's difficult later years overshadowed her former greatness; reviewing Nadine Cohodas's biography, he speaks of the difficulty of reading the final pages and concludes that "like so many of us who saw Simone onstage when she should have been convalescing or simply enjoying life, readers may feel an urgent need to listen to her old recordings to remind themselves of what they loved about her in the first place" (*The New York Times*, 12 February 2010, 12). Yet our access to those recordings is not as great as it could be.

The Purloined Voice

The "capricious behaviour" and "bizarre demands" associated with Simone tend to fall into two categories: those resulting from her disappointment with inattentive ("disrespectful") audiences and those resulting from her treatment at the hands of the music industry. Ironically, when Simone *is* recalled, she is often remembered for her hit 'My Baby Just Cares For Me', a song she not only thought was slight but which caused her considerable disappointment due to its having been part of her first disastrous record deal with Bethlehem Records in the 1950s, when she signed away for a paltry sum the rights to the material she recorded. In her later concerts, Simone invariably included 'My Baby . . .' in her set, often as an encore and often with an introduction such as that found on her *Live at Ronnie Scott's* recording: "I think this is what you've been waiting for". As Ian Penman notes, quoting a couplet from 'My Baby . . .', even as she sought to escape into song, this one song did not allow for escape:

> Singing, she remembers the dreams, reclaims some dignity.
> Sober, the daylight offends her eyes and remembrance has
> the sound of opening bomb hatches and what for latecom-
> ers are delights ("Even Lana Turner's smile/is something he
> can't see!") remain for her mnemonic daggers, reminders of
> rip-off and irrevocable loss, her own self-destructive airiness
> and ardour and spite (2003, 28).

For much of her career, Simone was painfully aware of the fact that her voice had been stolen from her and this awareness, combined with other issues that often clouded her mind, led her to behave in "irrational" ways. Lucy O'Brien describes waiting for an interview with Simone while the singer harangued her publicist for not making sure copies of Simone's autobiography were in the shops, ignoring the fact that the book had not yet been published. In another often cited example, Simone appeared on an American television chat show to promote *A Single Woman* and demanded to be paid then and there; following this incident, her current record label Elektra decided to drop her. In these examples, and numerous others, we witness Simone's fear of the theft of her voice articulated as diva-like behaviour.

Has Simone's voice been stolen, or is it better to think of it as having been purloined, recalling Edgar Allan Poe's famous tale of 'The Purloined Letter'

(1986, 330–49)? In the tale, a letter bearing a secret is stolen from a queen (at least, a "royal personage") and placed by the "purloiner" in a spot that is rendered invisible by its very visibility (it is in such an obvious place, the police do not think to look for it there). The story's plot, if not its connotations, resolves with the safe return of the letter to the queen by the detective Dupin. In making my comparison, I am thinking of Nina Simone as a "queen" (her preferred appellation[1]) whose voice is purloined and left in the open. In Poe's tale, the minister "hides" the incriminating document in the most obvious place, a card rack hanging from the mantelpiece. What more obvious place to "hide" Simone's purloined voice (and those of others) than in the overcrowded CD rack of a high street store? At the time of writing (although quite likely not for very much longer) those few remaining stores in the UK contain surprisingly large "Nina Simone" sections – surprising because the amount of music on offer seems to be in inverse proportion to the amount of Simone's music actually known or heard in or outside these stores. Her music is in full view (and within easy earshot), but not in its classic form, very often not in an artist-endorsed form and frequently in poorly recorded and packaged compilations. Our task might then become Dupin's: to return the purloined voice to its rightful place. Who gets to decide on that rightful place is, of course, a trickier matter.

Another way in which Simone has been purloined in the years since her death is via the remixing and sampling of her work. I began this book by reflecting on the remix of 'Sinnerman' that was released in 2003 by Felix da Housecat. It is interesting to consider the ways in which the sampled voices of musicians performing in traditional (or at least older) styles have been incorporated into newer styles of music-making. In Joseph Auner's (2003) discussion of "posthuman" voices, an example is given of Moby using Alan Lomax's field recordings of African American singers as textures of the "real" against which to project the synthetic sound of Moby's electronic music. In such a process the sampled voice runs the risk of being reduced to an ethnic and/or gendered and/or aged essence. This essentializing work is conducted by presenting the sampled voice as an authentic human voice within the machine. Felix's use of Simone's voice in the 'Sinnerman' remix similarly projects Simone as the authentic, human element in the mix while also giving her the job of articulating the song's lyric. In the case of 'Sinnerman', that lyric is an apocalyptic one from Simone's own particular brand of gospel-inspired posthumanism, thus connecting two seemingly distinct manifestations of the posthuman voice.

In 2007, another set of Simone remixes was released by the artist's former record label under the title *Nina Simone Remixed & Reimagined*. The blurb on the back of the CD praised Simone as a "spellbinding musical titan . . . revered today with an almost religious fervor". Introducing the new remixes as "Chill House or Lounge" (and thus adding to the numerous categories which have been attached to Simone's music over the years), the producers claim that "the clarion sound of the original diva has never seemed timelier for a troubled world eager to embrace the unbridled power of Nina Simone" (D4). There are some imaginative responses to the artist's work on the collection, for example Jephté Guillaume's guitar contribution to François K's remix of 'Here Comes the Sun' (which may be a tribute to George Harrison as much as Simone) and the electric sitar added to DJ Logic's reworking of 'Obeah Woman'. However, it is untrue to describe the result as presenting "the unbridled power" of Simone simply because the very act of remixing the work has placed a bridle upon it. In some of the tracks – Coldcut's "Save Me" and Tony Humphries's "Turn Me On", for example – the voice is reduced to a sampled loop, thus diminishing Simone's role while expanding that of the remixers. Thus reduced and disembodied, Simone enters the Afrofuturist present shorn of all her danger and vitality, a bit part in someone else's "futurhythmachine" (Eshun 1998) rather than the (pirate) captain of her own ship. The case for sampling as an archival practice, as presented in the earlier cited claims by Tricia Rose and Michael Dyson, remains strong. However, such accounts should also be balanced against the need to attend to the archive of Simone's own full-blooded, "unbridled" recordings.

We can posit various reasons for the difficulty in identifying a classic Nina Simone album. Each album, and especially those from her classic period (the "long 1960s"), showcases the diversity of her work, splitting apart notions of coherence. Record companies might have tried to suggest coherence with titles such as *Folksy Nina*, *Pastel Blues* and *Silk & Soul*, but the albums' contents invariably belied such attempts to fix the sound stylistically. Another reason is that Simone's classic period predates the time where *albums* by black artists outside the jazz sphere were conceived as works and where albums by female artists were similarly conceived (save, perhaps, in folk music). This is partly to do with racial categorizing, with record companies marketing black performers as singles artists, an assumption that would be challenged by the work of Marvin Gaye, Isaac Hayes, Curtis Mayfield, Funkadelic and other (predominantly male) artists of the late 1960s and early 1970s. However, the assumption lingered due to predominant ideas of the culture industry and critics during the period of popular music canonization, from the late 1960s through the 1970s, the same period that witnessed the ideology of the album as a "work".

In the twenty-first century, it may make little sense to speak of "albums". Simone's work, it could be argued, is prime playlist material for the iTunes age. We can pick and choose, categorize and reorganize, take the open text of her life and work and fashion it ("remixed and reimagined") to our own patterns in true postmodernist style. Will Friedwald makes a similar point in his appraisal of Simone's work, suggesting various themed playlists that would enable the listener to rediscover her work in a more coherent fashion: "*Simone sings Broadway* . . . songs with blues elements and blues associations . . . traditional spirituals and religious songs . . . traditional American and European songs . . . traditional music from the African diaspora . . ." (Friedwald 2010, 415).

But even when we think in terms of the playlist, there is still an ideology of the album at work and it is still, for better or worse, attached to critical appraisal. Simone deserves such appraisal. Her work needs to be written about *as* work. It seems difficult at this stage to imagine an extended study devoted to just one of Simone's albums, as Ashley Kahn has done for *Kind of Blue* and *A Love Supreme*, as David Quantick has done for the Beatles' "White Album", or as Continuum's 33⅓ series has done for many rock, pop and soul albums. It is perhaps easier to imagine such a process being applied to particular songs in a manner similar to David Margolick's account of 'Strange Fruit'; indeed, shorter articles have already devoted space to contextual studies of 'Mississippi Goddam', 'Four Women' and 'Pirate Jenny' (Lynskey 2010, Kernodle 2008, Brooks 2011). In this book, I have sketched some possible approaches to the study of Simone's songs and albums, though these are only preliminary accounts of what, in my opinion, deserve to be more extended works.

Conclusion

> All things are possible; the poor girl . . . can put on a silk gown and transform herself into an Empress; she can wear a lampshade-fringe-crown. There is the perception, on the one hand, of the blues as lowlife (the view of middle-class jazz fans and critics) and on the other hand, the blues as high life, royalty (classic blues singers and their fans). This combination can't be bettered: the result is a working-class Queen. No ordinary Queen who has inherited somebody else's lineage quite by chance, but a diva with style, daring, panache, imagination and talent. A Queen who knows how to shimmy. A Queen who can send herself up. A Queen who can holler and shout. A Queen who knows what it is all about. A Queen of Tragedy; a Queen of Bad Men; a Queen of the jailhouse (Kay 1997, 65–6).

> At times she has acted like the voice of pride or yearning. At times she has appeared as a diva, a symbol of national conscience, expressing rage and frustration. And she has always illuminated the byways of love, from the point of view of a strong woman. . . . She has embodied tragic heroines while questioning the necessity of tragedy (C4, liner notes).

Neither of these quotations is about Nina Simone, though they are not unconnected to her. The first refers to Bessie Smith, whose blues Simone channelled in her versions of 'Gimme a Pigfoot' and 'Nobody Knows You When You're Down and Out'; the second comes from Arto Lindsay's liner notes to Maria Bethânia's album *Canto do Pajé*, on which Simone appeared. Beyond these contingent connections, however, both descriptions seem to capture the qualities and contradictions of the subject of this book. Simone can and should be situated amongst a court of similarly royal, imperious, commanding female singers of the twentieth century, a list that would include Smith and Bethânia, as it would Billie Holiday, Dinah Washington, Maria Callas,

Edith Piaf, Judy Garland, Amália Rodrigues, Umm Kulthum, Fairuz and Mercedes Sosa. Simone shares the passion of these women and their tragedy, melancholy and unresolved yearning.

In this book, I have attempted to articulate the ways in which Nina Simone responded to various personal and cultural traumas, fashioning an art that dwelled on such seemingly contradictory topics as revolution and disappointment, utopia and dystopia, freedom's victory and the yearning for home. That she was able to do so was testimony to an authorial and active(ist) voice that became the centre of any material it attached itself to. Yet it is also important to stress that Simone's authority cast a spell of mourning and melancholy that often spoke of anything but freedom. I do not wish to think of her well-publicized difficulty as the down side of an otherwise inspiring freedom singer but rather as a reflection of a constitutive part of the freedom she sought, occasionally found and often lost.

Simone's was not a departure from symptom to cure but a journey through the dark night of the soul that illuminated, in its wake, the tragic betrayal of the progressive dream. If one were to map this journey, it could be laid out as follows: firstly, an attempt to speak the symbolic from the position of symbolic exclusion (roughly, late 1950s to late 1960s); secondly, a move into a performance of psychosis that railed against a radical loss (c. 1970 to late 1970s); finally, a kind of settled instability that veered, with some level of consistency, between mourning, melancholy and occasional victory (late 1970s to 2003). If Nina Simone, like Bob Dylan, reached a point where she no longer saw "the chimes of freedom flashing", this does not detract from the fact that she represented, and continues to represent for many, an example of just such a victorious sonic event. As witnesses to this event we need to prevent Simone's departure from becoming a symptomatic absence in the history of popular music and the wider culture.

I have evoked the name of Bob Dylan a number of times during this book because I feel that, in many ways, Dylan and Simone help to shed light on each other. Two "enduring enigmas", they provide often lucid, and just as often paradoxical, accounts of the subject's occupation of space, place and time. Dylan, seemingly the epitome of the artist who "don't look back", leaves a trail of regret, nostalgia and indecision as he moves down the highway, a suggestion that his forward-looking music is preoccupied with experience, memory and a longing for home (Elliott 2009). Simone, an artist who, I have suggested, moved increasingly towards an emphasis on experience, memory and loss, nevertheless maintained a sense of renewal and reinvention to the end of her career. We do not need to "remix and reimagine" her because, like Dylan, she was more than capable of doing this herself. Having noted, then, that the burden of the past weighs heavily on both these artists, I would like to close by focusing instead on the future in the form of becoming and renewal.

In an interview in the 1970s, Jonathan Cott questioned Dylan about sacrifice and renewal and suggested that the artist had made reinvention his mission: "To die before dying, shedding your skin, making new songs out of old ones". In response, Dylan cited his song 'It's Alright Ma (I'm Only Bleeding)': "That's my mission in life . . . 'He not busy being born is busy dying'" (Cott 2006, 264). In a more recent interview for Martin Scorsese's documentary *No Direction Home*, Dylan made a similar claim: "An artist has got to be careful never really to arrive at a place where he thinks he's at somewhere. You always have to realize that you're constantly in a state of becoming" (F6). These notions – shedding skin, being born, becoming – seem to me to describe Simone as well as they do Dylan. In Chapter 3, I referred to a live performance of 'I Wish I Knew How It Would Feel To Be Free' during which Simone improvised a sermon for her audience/congregation, quoting St. Paul on the transformation of the self via the renewal of thought or mind. Such transformations are evident throughout Simone's work, from the ways in which she challenged categorization to the ways in which she renewed and reinvented other people's songs as well as her own previous versions. Furthermore, reincarnation was a theme Simone returned to many times in her career, from her recording of Bernstein's 'Who Am I' in the 1960s to 'Fodder in Her Wings' in the 1980s and the references to being a reincarnated Egyptian queen that continued into the 1990s. Other songs spoke explicitly of new life: – 'Ain't Got No / I Got Life', 'Another Spring', 'Feeling Good'.

One could draw upon virtually any one of Simone's available performances to provide testimony of newness and reinvention. Because it has not been mentioned yet in this book and because it is a late album (1987), and therefore evidence of Simone's continued fidelity to renewal four decades into her career, I will select *Let It Be Me*. The album presents a live performance by Simone in a trio (Arthur Adams on guitar and electric bass, Cornell McFadden on drums) at the Vine St. Bar in Hollywood. In many ways the tracks represent tradition and golden oldies; the first track on the album is 'My Baby Just Cares For Me', while there is a distinct emphasis on the blues

('Sugar in My Bowl', 'Be My Husband'), gospel ('Balm in Gilead', 'If You Pray Right (Heaven Belongs to You)') and romantic love songs ('Let It Be Me', 'If You Knew'). Without 'Mississippi Goddam' or any spoken interventions from the artist, we seem to be presented with a rather sanitized Nina Simone. Yet the songs sound new and fresh due to the slightly unusual accompaniment; Adams's subtly insistent interventions provide an edge different to that heard on previous Simone recordings, while Simone's beautifully clear and flowing piano excursions crackle with new life. The track that really stands out, however – more than the radically altered take on Dylan's 'Just Like a Woman', or the return to Janis Ian's 'Stars' a decade on from Simone's unforgettable performance of the song at Montreux – is the six-minute version of 'Fodder on My Wings', the enigmatic title track from Simone's 1982 album. The original recording had been unusual instrumentally, opening with percussion and vocals that evoked Central African music, then moving to a harpsichord section before settling into the main song, for which Simone switched from harpsichord to piano (B8, track 2). Its strangeness was intensified with the addition of Simone's lyric, outlining the peregrinations of a reincarnated bird – clearly a metaphor for the artist herself – as "she flitted here and there / United States, everywhere". The ambiguous territory carved out by the song is echoed in the hybrid of musical styles: Bach via Brazzaville. The earlier version was very much a crafted, hybridized product whose studio construction was as interesting as the strange lyric of the bird "with fodder in her brain / and dust inside her wings". When performing the song at Ronnie Scott's in the mid-1980s, Simone started by using the harpsichord setting of an electronic keyboard and switched to piano midway through. For the Vine St. set, she plays piano throughout, providing a quite remarkable impression with her keyboard virtuosity (B13, track 3). By this time the lyric of the song has been corrected to "fodder in her wings / and dust inside her brain", switching the words around from earlier versions. The flitting bird has had extra places added to her itinerary, including Switzerland, France and England, making her even more obviously an avatar of Simone. The artist as reincarnated bird watches the people as she flits; she is external to them, above them, never at one with them. Even though we are told that this bird has fallen to Earth, the music promises freedom from terrestrial bonds. Although the occasional contributions of the stuttering bass seem too weighed down to ever take off, the piano is utterly liberated, beginning a solo at 2:45 that does not really resolve until the end of the song. Even as Simone resumes singing, repeating the song's verses and singing the refrain "how sad, how sad", her right hand keeps going, floating notes above the song in a manner that suggests all fodder, all baggage, has long been discarded. There is a sense – fleeting, perhaps, but resonant with affective possibility – that this is what freedom would feel like.

Notes

1 Categories

1 A certain amount of confusion surrounds both the title and the release date of Simone's first album. While most sources (including Simone's biographer Nadine Cohodas and Mauro Boscarol, the keeper of the diligently researched Nina Simone Database) cite the title as *Little Girl Blue* (item A1 in this book's Discography), the album has also been released with an identical cover as *Nina Simone* and *Jazz as Played in an Exclusive Side Street Club*, while the recordings themselves have reappeared on countless subsequent compilations, some based on the running order of the original album. I will refer to the album as *Little Girl Blue*, although the edition I have used is entitled *Jazz as Played in an Exclusive Side Street Club*, as released on CD by Charly (B12 in the Discography). See Cohodas (2010, 76–85) on the recording and release of the album and http://www.boscarol.com/ninasimone for Boscarol's database. Hereafter, recordings will be cited in the text as alphanumeric references. The reference (e.g. A1 or B12) refers to the item's location in the Discography and Videography at the end of the book.

2 For a more extensive description of "negative defining" or defining via alterity in music, see Elliott 2010, especially chapter 5.

3 Scott's genre-busting 78s can be heard on C31. Simone and Scott collaborated on some recordings which, to date, have only been released in limited form via Simone's former husband Andy Stroud. For more on Scott, see McGee (2009, 113–33). Interesting interviews with both Scott and Simone can be found in Taylor (1993).

4 Later, Odetta would develop a range of different voices, from operatic to lowdown blues, to deploy in the service of particular songs. For a taste of how both Odetta's style and folk music conventions had shifted by the end of the 1980s, listen to her performance of 'Children, Go Where I Send Thee' on D3; she sounds utterly possessed and her audience are suitably "sent" too. Odetta had displayed an earthier delivery at least by the time of *Odetta and the Blues* in 1962, suggesting that vocal expectations in folk began to change around the turn of that decade.

5 'Sinnerman' is available in different versions on B5, B10 and B16. My initial comments refer to the version available on B10 (originally released on A16), as do those of Middleton. This is the most famous version, the one that frequently appears on film and television soundtracks and which was part of the *Verve Remixed* project referred to in the Introduction (D5).

6 For more on the history of the Village Vanguard, see Gordon (1980). For an account of Bob Dylan's early career in Greenwich Village, see Dylan (2005).

2 Politics

1   CORE = Congress of Racial Equality (founded 1941); SCLC = Southern Christian Leader-ship Conference (founded 1957); SNCC = Student Nonviolent Coordinating Committee (founded 1960).

2   McGinn's version of 'Go Limp' can be heard on D1 (disc 1, track 7). The collection also features Simone's 'Mississippi Goddam' and many other songs addressing civil rights issues.

3   For reasons explained in the text, the following analysis of the three songs in the "Mar-tin Luther King Suite" is based on the versions included on B9.

3 Possession

1   The effectiveness of the intro has been somewhat damaged by a number of released versions where a mastering error removes the sound from one of the stereo channels. This error was rectified on C19. The initial description is based on this recording (track 10).

2   It is rewarding to compare Natacha Atlas's tour de force rendering of the song, which, seemingly influenced by Simone's version, combines the lush string sounds of Egyptian film music with driving percussion, electronics and multiple vocal interjections; Atlas does her own 'speaking in tongues' by mixing English and Arabic lyrics with scat-style vocables (C1, track 1). Perhaps the ultimate "possessed" performance to date has been that of Diamanda Galás, who looks to Screamin' Jay Hawkins rather than Simone for inspiration (C19, disc 2, track 3).

3   Robertson's own composition 'The Weight', included on the same album (C2, track 5), echoed the gospel mood by capturing a sense of religious mysticism and mythology in its lyrics and being structured in a classic "accumulative style" that would lend itself well to gospel singing. This aspect is made even more explicit in Cassandra Wilson's reading of the song (C40, track 1).

4   The dates given here are those of the best-known recordings of each performance. They can be found on the following albums. Collins: 1964, *#3*; 1966, *In My Life*; 1968, *Wildflowers* and *Who Knows Where The Time Goes*; 1969, 'Turn! Turn! Turn!' (7" single); 1994, *Judy Sings Dylan . . . Just Like A Woman*. Simone: 1964, *In Concert*; 1969, *To Love Somebody* and *Nina Simone & Piano!*; 1971, *Here Comes The Sun*; 1978, *Baltimore*. Flack: 1969, *First Take*; 1970, *Chapter Two*; 1971, *Quiet Fire*; 1973, *Killing Me Softly*.

5   In addition to the recorded performance listed here, Roberta Flack also performed Simone's 'Young, Gifted and Black' live, while Simone performed 'Compared to What', a track recorded by Flack. Although Flack claimed Simone as an influence, relations between the two were not always amicable (Nathan 1999).

6   There is no doubt some interesting cultural theoretical work to be done here with the notion of 'infection'. Certainly, a reading that proposes the way's Sinatra's theme song comes to be infected by a black female performer – which pays attention, in other words, to the racial and gendered implications of "infection" – would be worthwhile. Sid Vicious, of course, brought his own special brand of infection (and inflection) to the song later in the decade.

4 Lateness

1　The three songs of the "Martin Luther King Suite" can be heard on B19. The unedited version of 'Why? (The King of Love Is Dead)', with all of Simone's spoken comments, can be heard on B20.

2　I do not want to make a clear distinction here between individual biography and history, for, as is clear from any study of the careers of Hank Williams and Billie Holiday, it is because of historical circumstances that these performers aged so quickly and were able to articulate at an early age experiences which their contemporaries in more privileged social positions could not have dreamed about. The point here is rather to move between the biographical and historical in the manner alluded to earlier in this book.

3　Staying in the folk idiom, we might also want to compare both these songs to 'Bob Dylan's Dream', wherein the eponymous singer converts 'Lord Franklin', a ballad about a sailor lost at sea, to one about the lost friends of youth. The twenty-two-year-old Dylan, on a fast track to artistic success and popular music revolution, is found here wishing he were home with the friends of his youth (C11, track 8). Interestingly, according to Nat Hentoff's sleeve notes for the album, 'Bob Dylan's Dream' emerged from a conversation the even younger Dylan had with Oscar Brown Jr. Brown, of course, was the young black hope of Greenwich Village mentioned earlier, and the composer of a number of songs performed by Nina Simone such as 'Brown Baby', 'Work Song' and 'When Malindy Sings'.

4　Both songs were published in *Broadside* and are available on D1. In the accompanying notes (p. 78) Ian is quoted as saying she received bomb threats and razor blades in the post after recording the song.

5 Legacy

1　At the close of *La Légende*, Simone is heard saying, "Who am I? I'm a reincarnation of an Egyptian queen". The singer made numerous similar references during concerts (for example, the 1976 Montreux concert discussed in this book) and was often pictured in "regal" postures. The cover of *Fodder on My Wings* is an excellent example of this: Nina Simone as Cleopatra. See also her account of her appearance at New York's Town Hall (Simone and Cleary 2003, 66) and Penman's description of the numerous "Ninas", both quoted earlier.

Bibliography

Acker, Kerry. 2004. *Nina Simone*. Philadelphia: Chelsea House.

Adorno, Theodor W. 2002. *Essays on Music*, ed. Richard Leppert, trans. Susan H. Gillespie. Berkeley and London: University of California Press.

Agacinski, Sylviane. 2003. *Time Passing: Modernity and Nostalgia*, trans. Jody Gladding. New York: Columbia University Press.

Althusser, Louis. 2008. *On Ideology*. London and New York: Verso.

Anderson, Benedict. 1991. *Imagined Communities: Reflections on the Origin and Spread of Nationalism*, rev. edn. London and New York: Verso.

Auner, Joseph. 2003. "'Sing It for Me': Posthuman Ventriloquism in Recent Popular Music". *Journal of the Royal Musical Association* 128(1): 98–122.

Austin, John L. 1975. *How to Do Things with Words*, eds J. O. Urmson and Marina Sbisà. 2nd edn. Oxford: Clarendon Press.

Badiou, Alain. 2003. *Saint Paul: The Foundation of Universalism*, trans. Ray Brassier. Stanford, CA: Stanford University Press.

—— 2005. *Being and Event*, trans. Oliver Feltham. London and New York: Continuum.

Baldwin, James. [1963] 1971. *The Fire Next Time*. Harmondsworth: Penguin. Citations refer to the Penguin edition.

Benjamin, Walter. 2006. *Selected Writings Volume 4: 1938-1940*, eds Howard Eiland and Michael W. Jennings, trans. Edmund Jephcott et al. Cambridge, MA and London: The Belknap Press of Harvard University Press.

Berman, Russell A. 2004. "Sounds Familiar? Nina Simone's Performances of Brecht/Weill Songs". In *Sound Matters: Essays on the Acoustics of Modern German Culture*, eds Nora M. Alter and Lutz Koepnick, 171–82. New York and Oxford: Berghahn Books.

Bowman, Rob. 2003. "The Determining Role of Performance in the Articulation of Meaning: The Case of 'Try a Little Tenderness'". In *Analyzing Popular Music*, ed. Allan F. Moore, 103–30. Cambridge: Cambridge University Press.

Boym, Svetlana. 2001. *The Future of Nostalgia*. New York: Basic Books.

Brooks, Daphne A. 2011. "Nina Simone's Triple Play". *Callaloo* 34(1): 176–97.

Brun-Lambert, David. 2009. *Nina Simone: The Biography*. London: Aurum.

Butler, Judith. 1999. *Gender Trouble: Feminism and the Subversion of Identity*. 2nd ed. New York and London: Routledge.

—— 2004. *Precarious Life: The Powers of Mourning and Violence*. London and New York: Verso.

Carby, Hazel V. 1998. "It Jus Be's Dat Way Sometime: The Sexual Politics of Women's Blues". In *The Jazz Cadence of American Culture*, ed. Robert G. O'Meally, 470–83. New York: Columbia University Press.

Caruth, Cathy. 1995. "Introduction". In *Trauma: Explorations in Memory*, ed. Cathy Caruth, 3–12. Baltimore and London: Johns Hopkins University Press.

Cashmore, Ellis. 1997. *The Black Culture Industry*. London and New York: Routledge.

Cohodas, Nadine. 2010. *Princess Noire: The Tumultuous Reign of Nina Simone*. New York: Pantheon.

Collins, Judy. 2003. *Sanity and Grace: A Journey of Suicide, Survival, and Strength*. New York: Tarcher/Penguin.

Collins, Patricia Hill. 2009. *Black Feminist Thought: Knowledge, Consciousness, and the Politics of Empowerment*. New York and London: Routledge.

Cott, Jonathan, ed. 2006. *Dylan on Dylan: The Essential Interviews*. London: Hodder & Stoughton.

Davis, Angela Y. 1998. *Blues Legacies and Black Feminism: Gertrude "Ma" Rainey, Bessie Smith, and Billie Holiday*. New York: Pantheon.

Du Bois, W. E. B. [1903] 1996. *The Souls of Black Folk*. New York and London: Penguin. Citations refer to the Penguin edition.

Dunn, Leslie C. and Nancy A. Jones. 1994. "Introduction". In *Embodied Voices: Representing Female Voices in Western Culture*, eds Leslie C. Dunn and Nancy A. Jones, 1–13. Cambridge: Cambridge University Press.

Dylan, Bob. 2005. *Chronicles: Volume One*. London: Pocket Books.

Dyson, Michael Eric. 2003. *Open Mike: Reflections on Philosophy, Race, Sex, Culture and Religion*. New York: Basic Civitas.

Elliott, Richard. 2008a. "Loss, Memory and Nostalgia in Popular Song: Thematic Aspects and Theoretical Approaches". Doctoral thesis. Newcastle upon Tyne: Newcastle University.

—— 2008b. "Popular Music and/as Event: Subjectivity, Love and Fidelity in the Aftermath of Rock 'n' Roll". *Radical Musicology* 3, http://www.radical-musicology.org.uk.

—— 2009. "The Same Distant Places: Bob Dylan's Poetics of Place and Displacement". *Popular Music and Society* 32(2): 249–70.

—— 2010. *Fado and the Place of Longing: Loss, Memory and the City*. Farnham: Ashgate.

—— 2011. "Public Consciousness, Political Conscience and Memory in Latin American *Nueva Canción*". In *Music and Consciousness: Philosophical, Psychological and Cultural Perspectives*, eds David Clarke and Eric Clarke, 327–42. Oxford: Oxford University Press.

Ennis, Philip H. 1992. *The Seventh Stream: The Emergence of Rocknroll in American Popular Music*. Hanover and London: Wesleyan University Press.

Eshun, Kodwo. 1998. *More Brilliant than the Sun: Adventures in Sonic Fiction*. London: Quartet.

Eyerman, Ron. 2001. *Cultural Trauma: Slavery and the Formation of African American Identity*. Cambridge: Cambridge University Press.

Eyerman, Ron and Andrew Jamison. 1991. *Social Movements: A Cognitive Approach*. Cambridge: Polity Press.

—— 1998. *Music and Social Movements: Mobilizing Traditions in the Twentieth Century*. Cambridge: Cambridge University Press.

Feldstein, Ruth. 2005. "'I Don't Trust You Anymore': Nina Simone, Culture, and Black Activism in the 1960s". *Journal of American History* 91(4): 1349–79.

Fentress, James and Chris Wickham. 1992. *Social Memory*. Oxford: Blackwell.

Floyd, Samuel A, Jr. 1995. *The Power of Black Music: Interpreting its History from Africa to the United States*. Oxford and New York: Oxford University Press.

Foucault, Michel. 1979. "What is an Author?". In *Textual Strategies: Perspectives in Post-Structuralist Criticism*, ed. Josué V. Harari, 141–60. Ithaca, NY: Cornell University Press.

Freud, Sigmund. 1962. *The Standard Edition of the Complete Psychological Works of Sigmund Freud, Volume 3: Early Psycho-Analytic Publications*, trans. and ed. James Strachey. London: The Hogarth Press.

Friedwald, Will. 1997. *Sinatra! The Song is You: A Singer's Art*. New York: Da Capo Press.

—— 2010. *A Biographical Guide to the Great Jazz and Pop Singers*. New York: Pantheon.

Funkhouser, Christopher. 1995. "An Interview with Nathaniel Mackey". *Callaloo* 18(2): 321–34.

Gates, Henry Louis. 1988. *The Signifying Monkey: A Theory of African-American Literary Criticism*. Oxford and New York: Oxford University Press.

Gilroy, Paul. 1993. *The Black Atlantic: Modernity and Double Consciousness*. London and New York: Verso.

Gordon, Max. 1980. *Live at the Village Vanguard*. New York: St. Martin's Press.

Griffin, Farah Jasmine. 2001. *If You Can't Be Free, Be a Mystery: In Search of Billie Holiday*. New York: The Free Press.

—— 2004. "When Malindy Sings: A Meditation on Black Women's Vocality". In *Uptown Conversation: The New Jazz Studies*, eds Robert G. O'Meally, Brent Hayes Edwards and Farah Jasmine Griffin, 102–25. New York: Columbia University Press.

Guralnick, Peter. 1986. *Sweet Soul Music: Rhythm and Blues and the Southern Dream of Freedom*. London: Virgin.

Hamilton, Marybeth. 2007. *In Search of the Blues: Black Voices, White Visions*. London: Jonathan Cape.

Hampton, Sylvia and David Nathan. 2004. *Nina Simone: Break Down & Let It All Out*. London: Sanctuary.

Hayes, Eileen M. and Linda F. Williams, eds. 2007. *Black Women and Music: More than the Blues*. Urbana and Chicago: University of Illinois Press.

Heble, Ajay. 2000. *Landing on the Wrong Note: Jazz, Dissonance and Critical Practice*. New York and London: Routledge.

Hobson, Janell. 2008. "Everybody's Protest Song: Music as Social Protest in the Performances of Marian Anderson and Billie Holiday". *Signs* 33(2): 443–8.

Hoffman, Eva. 2011. *Time*. London: Profile.

hooks, bell. 1990. *Yearning: Race, Gender, and Cultural Politics*. Boston: South End Press.

Hughes, Langston. 1995. *The Collected Poems of Langston Hughes*, ed. Arnold Rampersad. New York: Vintage.

Jameson, Fredric. 2005. *Archaeologies of the Future: The Desire Called Utopia and Other Science Fictions*. London and New York: Verso.

Kasten, Roy. 2004. "Wild is the Wind". In *Da Capo Best Music Writing 2004*, ed. Mickey Hart and Paul Bresnick, 145–8. Cambridge, MA: Da Capo.

Kay, Jackie. 1997. *Bessie Smith*. Bath: Absolute Press.

Kelley, Robin D. G. 1996. *Race Rebels: Culture, Politics, and the Black Working Class*. New York: Free Press.

—— 1997. *Yo' Mama's Disfunktional! Fighting the Culture Wars in Urban America*. Boston: Beacon Press.

Kernodle, Tammy. 2008. "'I Wish I Knew How It Would Feel to Be Free': Nina Simone and the Redefining of the Freedom Song of the 1960s". *Journal of the Society for American Music* 2(3): 295–317.

Lacan, Jacques. 2006. *Écrits*, trans. Bruce Fink. New York and London: Norton.

Leppert, Richard and George Lipsitz. 1990. "'Everybody's Lonesome for Somebody': Age, the Body and Experience in the Music of Hank Williams". *Popular Music* 9(3): 259–74.

Lischer, Richard. 1995. *The Preacher King: Martin Luther King, Jr. and the Word that Moved America*. New York and Oxford: Oxford University Press.

Lynskey, Dorian. 2010. *33 Revolutions per Minute: A History of Protest Songs*. London: Faber and Faber.

Maalouf, Amin. 2000. *On Identity*, trans. Barbara Bray. London: Harvill.

Margolick, David. 2002. *Strange Fruit: Billie Holiday, Café Society, and an Early Cry for Civil Rights*. Edinburgh: Canongate.

McGee, Kristen A. 2009. *Some Liked It Hot: Jazz Women in Film and Television, 1928–1959*. Middletown, CT: Wesleyan University Press.

Middleton, Richard. 2006. *Voicing the Popular: On the Subjects of Popular Music*. New York and London: Routledge.

Monson, Ingrid. 2007. *Freedom Sounds: Civil Rights Call Out to Jazz and Africa*. Oxford: Oxford University Press.

Moore, John. 1989. "'The Hieroglyphics of Love': The Torch Singers and Interpretation". *Popular Music* 8(1): 31–58.

Mowitt, John. 2002. *Percussion: Drumming, Beating, Striking*. Durham and London: Duke University Press.

Nathan, David. 1999. *The Soulful Divas*. New York: Billboard.

Neal, Mark Anthony. 1999. *What the Music Said: Black Popular Music and Black Public Culture*. New York and London: Routledge.

—— 2003. "Nina Simone: She Cast a Spell – and Made a Choice". *SeeingBlack.com*, http://www.seeingblack.com/2003/x060403/nina_simone.shtml.

Nora, Pierre. 1996. "General Introduction: Between Memory and History". In *Realms of Memory: Rethinking the French Past. Vol. 1: Conflicts and Divisions*. Directed by Pierre Nora, ed. Lawrence D. Kritzman, trans. Arthur Goldhammer, 1–20. New York: Columbia University Press.

O'Brien, Lucy. 2002. *She Bop II: The Definitive History of Women in Rock, Pop and Soul*. London and New York: Continuum.

Patterson, Orlando. 1998. *Rituals of Blood: The Consequences of Slavery in Two American Centuries*. Washington, DC: Basic Civitas.

Penman, Ian. 2003. "Always Searching for a Key". *The Wire* 232, June: 26–8.

Peterson, Richard A. 1990. "Why 1955? Explaining the Advent of Rock Music". *Popular Music* 9(1): 97–116.

—— 1998. "The Dialectic of Hard-Core and Soft-Shell Country Music". In *Reading Country Music: Steel Guitars, Opry Stars and Honky-Tonk Bars*, ed. Cecilia Tichi, 234–55. Durham, NC and London: Duke University Press.

Poe, Edgar Allan. 1986. *The Fall of the House of Usher and Other Writings*, ed. David Galloway. Harmondsworth: Penguin.

Poizat, Michel. 1992. *The Angel's Cry: Beyond the Pleasure Principle in Opera*, trans. Arthur Denner. Ithaca, NY and London: Cornell University Press.

Ritchie, Jean. 1997. *Folk Songs of the Southern Appalachians*. 2nd edn. Lexington: University Press of Kentucky.

Robins, Kevin. 2005. "Identity". In *New Keywords: A Revised Vocabulary of Culture and Society*, eds Tony Bennett, Lawrence Grossberg and Meaghan Morris, 172–5. Oxford: Blackwell.

Rose, Tricia. 1994. *Black Noise: Rap Music and Black Culture in Contemporary America*. Hanover, NH: Wesleyan University Press.

Russell, Michelle. 1982. "Slave Codes and Liner Notes". In *But Some of Us Are Brave: Black Women's Studies*, eds Gloria T. Hull, Patricia Bell Scott and Barbara Smith, 129–40. New York: The Feminist Press.

Russell, Tony. 2001. "Blacks, Whites and Blues". In *Yonder Come the Blues: The Evolution of a Genre*, by Paul Oliver et al., 143–242. Cambridge: Cambridge University Press.

Said, Edward W. 2005. *On Late Style: Music and Literature Against the Grain*. London: Bloomsbury.

Santner, Eric L. 1990. *Stranded Objects: Mourning, Memory, and Film in Postwar Germany*. Ithaca, NY and London: Cornell University Press.

Sidran, Ben. [1971] 1995. *Black Talk: How the Music of Black America Created a Radical Alternative to the Values of Western Literary Tradition*. Edinburgh: Payback Press. Citations refer to the Payback edition.

Simone, Nina and Stephen Cleary. [1991] 2003. *I Put a Spell On You: The Autobiography of Nina Simone*. New York: Da Capo Press. Citations refer to the Da Capo edition.

Small, Christopher. 1998. *Musicking: The Meanings of Performing and Listening*. Middletown, CT: Wesleyan University Press.

Spillers, Hortense J. 2003. *Black, White, and in Color: Essays on American Literature and Culture*. Chicago: University of Chicago Press.

Spitzer, Michael. 2006. *Music as Philosophy: Adorno and Beethoven's Late Style*. Bloomington, IN: Indiana University Press.

Taylor, Arthur. 1993. *Notes and Tones: Musician-to-Musician Interviews*. New York: Da Capo.

Van Deburg, William L. 1992. *New Day in Babylon: The Black Power Movement and American Culture, 1965–1975*. Chicago and London: University of Chicago Press.

Ward, Brian. 1998. *Just My Soul Responding: Rhythm and Blues, Black Consciousness, and Race Relations*. London: UCL Press.

Weheliye, Alexander G. 2002. "Posthuman Voices in Contemporary Black Popular Music". *Social Text* 20(2): 21–47.

— 2005. *Phonographies: Grooves in Sonic Afro-Modernity*. Durham, NC: Duke University Press.

Williams, Richard. 2009. *The Blue Moment: Miles Davis's* Kind of Blue *and the Remaking of Modern Music*. London: Faber and Faber.

Young, Kevin. 2003. "Introduction". In *Blues Poems*, ed. Kevin Young. London: Everyman's Library.

Discography and videography

The Discography/Videography is divided into six sections: (A) a list of original albums released during Nina Simone's career, excluding compilations which collected previously released material, arranged chronologically for a general overview of Simone's "official" recorded legacy; (B) recordings by Nina Simone used in researching and writing this book, including "2-on-1" CD reissues, compilations and box sets, arranged alphabetically; (C) recordings by other artists; (D) Various Artist compilations; (E) broadcasts; (F) video recordings. Catalogue details are given for all items in sections (B), (C), (D) and (F). All items in sections (B), (C) and (D) are CDs unless otherwise indicated. Dates in square brackets indicate original release date if different to the edition listed. Each item is numbered to match the alphanumeric references used throughout the book (e.g. A1, B12). For a full interactive discography, readers are directed to Mauro Boscarol's well-researched Nina Simone Database at http://www.boscarol.com/ninasimone.

(A) Original albums released during Nina Simone's career (listed chronologically and divided by record label)

Bethlehem
A1. *Little Girl Blue* [also known as *Jazz as Played in an Exclusive Side Street Club*] (1958)
A2. *And Her Friends* [collaborative album containing only four tracks by Simone] (1960)

Colpix
A3. *The Amazing Nina Simone* (1959)
A4. *At Town Hall* (1959)
A5. *At Newport* (1960)
A6. *Forbidden Fruit* (1961)
A7. *At The Village Gate* (1962)
A8. *Sings Ellington* (1962)

A9. *Nina's Choice* [compilation of single releases] (1963)
A10. *At Carnegie Hall* (1963)
A11. *Folksy Nina* [with material from Carnegie Hall] (1964)
A12. *Nina Simone With Strings* [adds strings to earlier recordings] (1966)

Philips
A13. *In Concert* (1964)
A14. *Broadway-Blues-Ballads* (1964)
A15. *I Put a Spell on You* (1965)
A16. *Pastel Blues* (1966)
A17. *Let It All Out* (1966)
A18. *Wild Is the Wind* (1966)
A19. *High Priestess of Soul* (1967)

RCA
A20. *Sings the Blues* (1967)
A21. *Silk & Soul* (1967)
A22. *'Nuff Said* (1968)
A23. *Nina Simone and Piano!* (1969)
A24. *To Love Somebody* (1969)
A25. *Black Gold* (1970)
A26. *Here Comes the Sun* (1971)
A27. *Emergency Ward!* (1972)
A28. *It Is Finished* (1974)

Stroud
A29. *Gifted & Black* (1971)
A30. *Nina Simone Sings Billie Holiday* (1972)
A31. *Gospel According to Nina Simone* (1973)
A32. *Live at Berkeley* (1973)

Various labels
A33. *Baltimore*, CTI (1978)
A34. *Fodder on My Wings*, Carrère (1982)
A35. *Nina's Back*, VPI (1985)
A36. *Live & Kickin'*, VPI (1987)
A37. *Let It Be Me*, Verve (1987)
A38. *A Single Woman*, Elektra (1993)

(B) Nina Simone albums used for this book (A–Z by title)

B1. *The Amazing Nina Simone*. EMI 724347320620, 2005.

B2. *At Carnegie Hall*. EMI 724347322129, 2005.

B3. *At Newport*. EMI 724347321627, 2005.

B4. *At Town Hall*. EMI 724347321528, 2005.

B5. *At the Village Gate*. EMI 724347321825, 2005.

B6. *Baltimore*. Epic/Legacy 5127912, 2001.

B7. *Emergency Ward / It Is Finished / Black Gold*. Camden 74321924802, 2002.

B8. *Fodder on My Wings*. Cy Records/Sunnyside SSC 1144, 2005.

B9. *Forever Young, Gifted & Black: Songs of Freedom and Spirit*. RCA/Legacy 82876744132, 2006.

B10. *Four Women: The Nina Simone Philips Recordings*. Verve 065021-2, 2003.

B11. *Gifted & Black / Live at Berkeley*. Charly SNAP300CD, 2009.

B12. *Jazz as Played in an Exclusive Side Street Club*. Charly SNAP 216CD, 2002.

B13. *Let It Be Me*. Verve 831437-2, 1990.

B14. *Nina's Back*. Magnum Music MM 059, 2000.

B15. *Nina Simone and Piano! / Silk & Soul*. Camden 74321698812, 1999.

B16. *Nina Simone Sings Billie Holiday / Gospel According to Nina Simone*. Charly SNAP288CD, 2007.

B17. *A Single Woman*. "Elektra Masters" edition. Elektra / Rhino 8122-79999-0, 2008.

B18. *Sings the Blues / 'Nuff Said*. Camden 74321869672, 2001.

B19. *Sugar in My Bowl: The Very Best of Nina Simone 1967–1972*. RCA 07863676352, 1998.

B20. *Tell It Like It Is: Rarities and Unreleased Recordings 1967–1973*. Sony BMG 88697056822, 2008.

B21. *To Be Free: The Nina Simone Story*. RCA/Legacy 88697381922, 2008.

B22. *To Love Somebody / Here Comes the Sun*. Camden 74321924792, 2002.

B23. *The Tomato Collection*. Tomato TOM-3005, 2002.

(C) Recordings by other artists (A–Z by artist)

C1. Atlas, Natacha. *Ayeshteni*. Mantra/EMI 7243 8101662 6, 2001.

C2. Band, The. *Music from Big Pink*. Capitol/EMI 724352539024, 2000 [1968].

C3.   Belafonte, Harry. *Belafonte at Carnegie Hall: The Complete Concert.* LP, RCA Starcall DHY0003, n.d. [reissue of 1959 recording].

C4.   Bethânia, Maria. *Canto do Pajé.* Verve 848508-2, 1990.

C5.   Brothers & Sisters, The. *Dylan's Gospel.* Sequel NEMCD 404, 2000 [1971].

C6.   Brown Jr., Oscar. *Sin and Soul . . . And Then Some.* Columbia/Legacy CK64994, 1996.

C7.   Cohen, Leonard. *Songs of Leonard Cohen.* Columbia/Legacy 88697 04742 2, 2007 [1967].

C8.   Collins, Judy. *Fifth Album / In My Life.* Elektra / Rhino 812273392-2, 2006.

C9.   Collins, Judy. *Wildflowers / Who Knows Where the Time Goes.* Elektra / Rhino 8122 73393-2, 2006.

C10. Coltrane, John. *The Complete 1961 Village Vanguard Recordings.* 4CD, Impulse! IMPD4-232, 1997.

C11. Dylan, Bob. *The Freewheelin' Bob Dylan.* Columbia CD 32390, 1989.

C12. Evans, Kellylee. *Nina.* Plus Loin PL4528, 2010.

C13. Exuma. *Exuma.* Mercury / Repertoire REPUK 1006, 2003 [1970].

C14. Fairport Convention. *What We Did on Our Holidays.* Island IMCD 294, 2003 [1969].

C15. Fairport Convention. *Unhalfbricking.* Island IMCD 61, 1990 [1969].

C16. Flack, Roberta. *First Take.* Atlantic 7567-82792-2, 1995 [1969].

C17. Flack, Roberta. *Killing Me Softly.* Atlantic 7567-87793-2, 1995 [1973].

C18. François, Claude. *Claude François.* Mercury France 536 158-2, 2000 [1967].

C19. Galás, Diamanda. *La Serpenta Canta.* Mute CDSTUMM206, 2003.

C20. Holcomb, Roscoe. *The High Lonesome Sound.* Smithsonian Folkways, SFCD 40104, 1998.

C21. Holiday, Billie. *Lady Day: The Very Best of.* Columbia MOOD52, 1997.

C22. Ian, Janis. *Stars & Aftertones.* Edsel EDSD 2044, 2010.

C23. Jungr, Barb. *Just Like a Woman (Hymn to Nina).* Linn AKD309, 2008.

C24. Kitt, Eartha. *My Way: A Musical Tribute to Rev. Martin Luther King, Jr.* Basic 50015, 1996 [1987].

C25. Kweli, Talib & Hi-Tek. *Reflection Eternal: Train of Thought.* Rawkus/EMI 072435 26143 25, 2000.

C26. Last Poets, The. *The Last Poets / This Is Madness.* Charly SNAX637CD, 2011.

C27. Lincoln, Abbey. *Straight Ahead.* Candid CCD79015, 1990 [1961].

C28. Odetta. *The Tin Angel.* Fantasy OBCCD-565-2, 1993 [1954].

C29. Roach, Max. *We Insist! Freedom Now Suite.* Poll Winners PWR27262, 2011 [1960].

C30. Scott, Hazel. *Relaxed Piano Moods.* Debut/Original Jazz Classics OJCCD-1702-2, 1992.

C31. Scott, Hazel. *The Chronological Classics 1946–1947.* Chronological Classics 1448, 2007.

C32. Seeger, Pete. *We Shall Overcome: The Complete Carnegie Hall Concert.* Columbia C2K 45312, 1989.

C33. Simone. *Simone on Simone.* Koch KOC-CD-4494, 2008.

C34. Sinatra, Frank. *My Way.* Reprise 7599-27049-2, c.1990 [1969].

C35. Sinatra, Frank. *A Man Alone: The Words & Music of McKuen.* Reprise 7599-27050-2, c.1990 [1969].

C36. Sinatra, Frank. *Watertown.* Reprise 9362-45689-2, c.1990 [1969].

C37. Taylor, Billy. *I Wish I Knew How It Would Feel To Be Free.* LP, Tower 5111, 1967.

C38. Waters, Patty. *Sings.* ESP-Disk ESP 1025, 2009 [1966].

C39. White, Kitty. *Cold Fire! & Folk Songs.* Fresh Sound FSR-CD 509, 2008.

C40. Wilson, Cassandra. *Belly of the Sun.* Blue Note 724353507220, 2002.

(D) Various artist compilations, soundtracks and cast recordings (A–Z by title)

D1. *The Best of Broadside 1962–1988: Anthems of the American Underground from the Pages of Broadside Magazine.* CD and book, Smithsonian Folkways SFWCD 40130, 2000.

D2. *Black Nativity – Gospel on Broadway: Original cast Recording.* LP, Vee Jay VJLP5022, c. 1962.

D3. *Fast Folk Musical Magazine.* Smithsonian Folkways, 1989.

D4. *Nina Simone Remixed & Reimagined.* RCA/Legacy 88697059272, 2007.

D5. *Verve Remixed.* Verve 0602498603031, 2003.

D6. *Voodoo Blues: The Devil Within.* NOT2CD360, 2010.

(E) Broadcasts

E1. 'Feeling Good: The Nina Simone Story'. Two-part radio programme presented by Simone (Lisa Stroud). Part One broadcast 4 January 2011 on BBC Radio 2. Part Two broadcast 11 January 2011 on BBC Radio 2.

(F) Video recordings

F1.   *La Légende.* Directed by Frank Lords (France/UK, 1992) DVD, Quantum Leap, 2002.

F2.   *Nina.* Directed by Joel Gold (USA, 1970). DVD included with the box set *To Be Free: The Nina Simone Story.* RCA / Legacy 88697381922, 2008.

F3.   *Nina Simone Live at Montreux 1976.* DVD, Montreux Sounds/Eagle Rock EREDV520, 2006.

F4.   *Nina Simone Live at Ronnie Scott's.* DVD, DD Home Entertainment DD07858, 2004.

F5.   *Nina Simone Live in '65 & '68.* DVD, Jazz Icons/Naxos 2.119014, 2008.

F6.   *No Direction Home: Bob Dylan.* Directed by Martin Scorsese. DVD. Spitfire Pictures, Grey Water Park Productions, 2005.

Index